Modeling and Control of Autonomous Systems

Edited by Mahmut Reyhanoglu

Published in London, United Kingdom

Modeling and Control of Autonomous Systems
http://dx.doi.org/10.5772/intechopen.1003384
Edited by Mahmut Reyhanoglu

Contributors
Alexandru Forrai, Amit Gali, Andrew F. Burke, Christina Nikolova, Jeroen Ploeg, Jingyuan Zhao, Mahmut Reyhanoglu, Mohammad Jafari, Mohsen Alirezaei, Tajinder Singh, Valentin Penev

First published in London, United Kingdom, 2025 by IntechOpen
IntechOpen is the global imprint of INTECHOPEN LIMITED, registered in England and Wales, registration number: 11086078, 167-169 Great Portland Street, London, W1W 5PF, United Kingdom

For EU product safety concerns: IN TECH d.o.o., Prolaz Marije Krucifikse Kozulić 3, 51000 Rijeka, Croatia, info@intechopen.com or visit our website at intechopen.com.

British Library Cataloguing-in-Publication Data
A catalogue record for this book is available from the British Library

Modeling and Control of Autonomous Systems
Edited by Mahmut Reyhanoglu
p. cm.
Print ISBN 978-1-83634-392-9
Online ISBN 978-1-83634-391-2
eBook (PDF) ISBN 978-1-83634-393-6

Meet the editor

Mahmut Reyhanoglu is currently a professor in the School of Engineering at Wentworth Institute of Technology (WIT) in Massachusetts, USA. Prior to joining the WIT, he held academic positions in various institutions, including Columbus State University in Columbus, Georgia, the University of North Carolina at Asheville, and Embry-Riddle Aeronautical University in Daytona Beach, Florida. His extensive research makes use of advanced mathematical techniques and models that arise from fundamental physical principles. His primary research interests are in the areas of nonlinear dynamical systems and control theory, with particular emphasis on applications to mechanical and aerospace systems, robotics and mechatronics. He has edited 6 books and authored/co-authored 6 book chapters, as well as over 140 peer-reviewed journal/proceedings papers. He served on the IEEE Transactions on Automatic Control Editorial Board and the IEEE Control Systems Society Conference Editorial Board as an Associate Editor. He also served as an International Program Committee member for several conferences and as a member of the AIAA Guidance, Navigation, and Control Technical Committee. He is currently serving as an editor of the International Journal of Aerospace Engineering and the MDPI Electronics Journal.

Contents

Preface

There has been considerable excitement recently over the emergence of new techniques for modeling and control of autonomous systems, defined as systems that function in complex environments with a high degree of independence. To operate autonomously, these systems rely on various sensor technologies that provide the necessary information on their surroundings for making data-driven decisions. The decision-making processes are guided by models and algorithms that predict physical and environmental dynamics. This book reviews recent advancements in modeling and control of autonomous systems, including autonomous vehicles operating in air, land, and sea with limited human supervision.

Chapter 1 is an introductory chapter, which briefly describes the sensing and control of autonomous robotic systems. In particular, it provides an overview of autonomous navigation in GPS-denied environments, such as dense urban areas, indoor or subterranean spaces.

Chapter 2 presents a learning-enhanced robust control framework for a broad class of nonlinear autonomous systems whose dynamics can be expressed in a feedback linearizable form. Four examples have been considered: control of a 2-DOF helicopter system, control of a PPR manipulator, control of an electric pump for liquid-propellant rocket engines, and control of thermoacoustic oscillations.

Chapter 3 is devoted to autonomously detecting radiation from ground targets using a fleet of fixed-wing tandem Unmanned Aerial Vehicles (UAVs). The control strategy proposed here is model-based, utilizing inverse dynamics and path-following algorithms.

Chapter 4 explores intelligent transport systems (ITSs), which improve transport operations, promote sustainable mobility, and deliver advantages such as greater productivity, enhanced safety, and reductions in time, cost, and energy consumption. ITSs integrate telecommunications, electronics, and information technologies with transport engineering to support the planning, design, operation, and management of transportation networks.

Chapter 5 provides an overview of deep learning applications in planning and control for autonomous vehicles. By incorporating adaptability and real-time responsiveness, deep learning has significantly advanced these areas within autonomous systems. Additionally, trajectory prediction models, particularly those utilizing recurrent neural networks, accurately forecast the movements of nearby objects.

Finally, Chapter 6 introduces Siemens' autonomy workflow and toolchain for testing and virtually validating Advanced Driver Assistance Systems (ADAS) and Autonomous Vehicle (AV) functions. It highlights the expanding ADAS and AV markets, driven by the integration of cutting-edge technologies and increasing global demand. Additionally, the chapter addresses key challenges in AV development, such as ensuring scalability, enhancing testing efficiency, and overcoming infrastructure limitations. It emphasizes the importance of Software-in-the-Loop (SIL) and Hardware-in-the-Loop (HIL) simulation environments as critical components of the verification and validation workflow.

Mahmut Reyhanoglu, Ph.D.
School of Engineering,
Wentworth Institute of Technology,
Boston, Massachusetts, USA

Chapter 1

Introductory Chapter: Modeling and Control of Autonomous Systems

Mahmut Reyhanoglu

1. Introduction

Systems that function in complex environments with a high degree of independence are defined as autonomous systems. These systems include robotic systems, cyber-physical systems, networked and distributed systems, and the Internet of Things (IoT). Increasingly, society depends on autonomous systems to perform complex tasks with minimal human intervention. Artificial intelligence (AI) enables these systems to learn from uncertain and unmodeled environments and make intelligent, independent decisions. To operate autonomously, these systems rely on various sensor technologies that provide the necessary information on their surroundings for making data-driven decisions. The decision-making processes are guided by models and algorithms that predict physical and environmental dynamics. This chapter aims to present a brief overview of the modeling, design, sensing, and control of autonomous robotic systems.

2. Unmanned autonomous robotic systems

The field of unmanned robotic systems is rapidly expanding, with a growing number of emerging applications. Examples of autonomous robotics systems include autonomous vehicles operating in space, air, land, and sea with limited human supervision [1–4]. Autonomous robots are particularly well-suited for tasks such as rescue operations in environments that are difficult or dangerous for humans to access. One notable development in this area is swarm robotics, where multiple robots collaborate to accomplish a common goal. For instance, a networked group of mobile robots can coordinate a search operation to detect hazardous emissions. Researchers have designed intelligent control algorithms to govern these robotic swarms [5].

Among unmanned systems, unmanned aerial vehicles (UAVs)—commonly known as drones—have seen a significant rise in use. In particular, quadrotor drones have gained popularity due to their enhanced maneuverability and versatility compared to fixed-wing UAVs. Their simple mechanical structure, relatively low cost, and compact size make them attractive for a wide range of applications. These applications include both military and civilian missions such as search and rescue, aerial mapping, surveillance, wildlife monitoring, and infrastructure inspection. Many of these tasks involve large-scale visual data acquisition, a capability supported by advances in image recognition technologies.

IntechOpen

Controlling UAVs presents complex challenges, as they are inherently nonlinear and strongly coupled systems. Traditional linearization-based control strategies may fall short in meeting performance demands, especially under disturbances, significant nonlinearities and uncertainties in system parameters. To address these challenges, control engineers have developed robust nonlinear control techniques.

One such technique is sliding mode control, known for its robustness against model uncertainties [6, 7]. In recent years, various nonlinear control strategies have been proposed to ensure stable and reliable operation of quadrotor UAVs over a wide range of conditions. These include feedback linearization, dynamic inversion, adaptive control, model-predictive control, neural network techniques, passivity-based approaches, fuzzy logic control, and learning-enabled control [8–17]. These methods aim to enhance control precision and system resilience in the face of complex flight dynamics and external disturbances.

3. Autonomous navigation in GPS-denied environments

In GPS-denied environments, such as dense urban areas and indoor or subterranean spaces, unmanned aerial systems (UAS) rely on a combination of sensors to navigate and maintain control. These sensors help UAS maintain stability, orientation, and position without relying on GPS signals. Some key sensors used in such scenarios include inertial measurement unit (IMU), visual odometry, light detection and ranging (LiDAR), radio detection and ranging (Radar), ultrasonic sensors, magnetometers, thermal and infrared (IR) sensors, and barometers [18].

The integration of simultaneous localization and mapping (SLAM) techniques allows for the creation of detailed maps needed for obstacle avoidance and path planning. Multi-sensor fusion techniques employ filters, such as extended Kalman filter (EKF), unscented Kalman filter (UKF), and particle filter, for reliably predicting the state of the UAS despite the sensor noise.

OptiTrack cameras are particularly useful in GPS-denied environments when precise position tracking is needed, especially indoors or in highly controlled outdoor

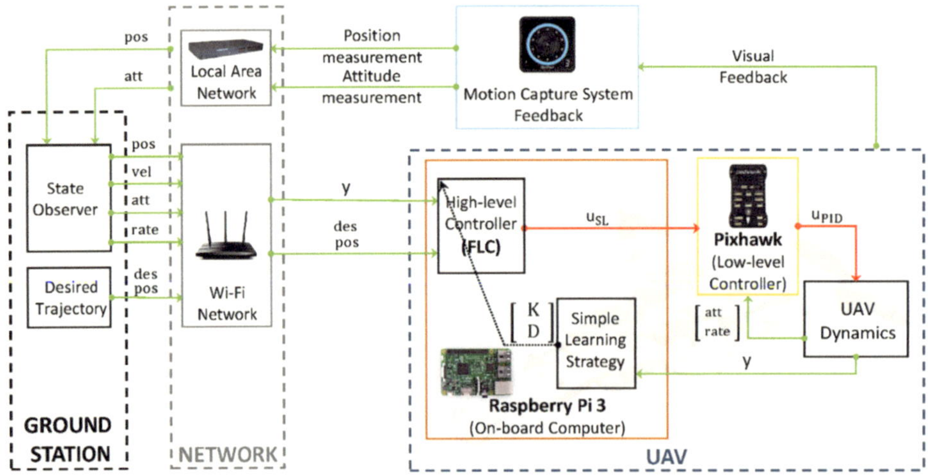

Figure 1.
A UAV control system with ground station interaction, motion capture system for visual feedback, and onboard processing via *Raspberry Pi.*

Figure 2.
A Robotics Motion Tracking Center (MTC) that allows for autonomous indoor operation of ground and air robotics systems in a GPS-denied environment. The Robotics MTC consists of 16 PrimeX 13W Opti-Track cameras and supporting hardware.

environments. They provide very high-precision tracking for applications like motion capture, robotics, and testing UAS in environments where GPS signals are unavailable. It works in conjunction with other sensors (like IMUs) for more robust navigation in certain scenarios but generally does not provide a complete solution for outdoor, large-area navigation in real-world conditions. A schematic diagram of a UAV control system with an OptiTrack motion capture system for visual feedback is given in **Figure 1**. A Robotics Motion Tracking Center (MTC) that allows for autonomous indoor operation of ground and air robotics systems in a GPS-denied environment is shown in **Figure 2**.

Author details

Mahmut Reyhanoglu
Wentworth Institute of Technology, Boston, Massachusetts, USA

*Address all correspondence to: mreyhanoglu@icloud.com

References

[1] Hajiahmadi F, Jafari M, Reyhanoglu M. Machine learning-based control of autonomous vehicles for solar panel cleaning systems in agricultural solar farms. AgriEngineering. 2024;**6**:1417-1435

[2] Kinaci MO, Bayezit I, Reyhanoglu M. A practical feedforward speed control for autonomous underwater vehicles. Ocean Engineering. 2020;**218**:108214

[3] Reyhanoglu M. Exponential stabilization of an underactuated autonomous surface vessel. IFAC Journal Automatica. 1997;**33**:2249-2254

[4] Jafari M, Xu H. Intelligent control for unmanned aerial systems with system uncertainties and disturbances using artificial neural network. Drones. 2018;**2**:30

[5] Reyhanoglu M. Unmanned Robotics Systems and Applications. London, UK: InTech; 2020. ISBN: 978-1-78984-566-2

[6] Kayacan E. Sliding mode learning control of uncertain nonlinear systems with Lyapunov stability analysis. Transactions of the Institute of Measurement and Control. 2019;**41**:1750-1760

[7] Topalov AV, Kaynak O. Online learning in adaptive neurocontrol schemes with a sliding mode algorithm. IEEE Transactions on Systems, Man, and Cybernetics, Part B Cybernetics. 2001;**31**:445-450

[8] Kayacan E, Kayacan E, Ramon H, Saeys W. Learning in centralized nonlinear model predictive control: Application to an autonomous tractor-trailer system. IEEE Transactions on Control Systems Technology. 2015;**23**:197-205

[9] Fu C, Hong W, Zhang L, Guo X, Tian Y. Adaptive robust backstepping attitude control for a multi-rotor unmanned aerial vehicle with time-varying output constraints. Aerospace Science and Technology. 2018;**78**:593-603

[10] Wu B, Wu J, He W, Tang G, Zhao Z. Adaptive neural control for an uncertain 2-DOF helicopter system with unknown control direction and actuator faults. Mathematics. 2022;**10**:4342

[11] Xu Z, Li W, Wang Y. Robust learning control for shipborne manipulator with fuzzy neural network. Frontiers in Neurorobotics. 2019;**13**:11

[12] Kayacan E, Khanesar MA, Rubio-Hervas J, Reyhanoglu M. Learning control of fixed-wing unmanned aerial vehicles using fuzzy neural networks. International Journal of Aerospace Engineering. 2017;**2017**:5402809

[13] Jafari M, Xu H, Garcia Carrillo LR. A neurobiologically-inspired intelligent trajectory tracking control for unmanned aircraft systems with uncertain system dynamics and disturbance. Transactions of the Institute of Measurement and Control. 2019;**41**:417-432

[14] Reyhanoglu M, Jafari M. A simple learning approach for robust tracking control of a class of dynamical systems. Electronics. 2023;**12**:2026

[15] Jafari M, Reyhanoglu M, Kozhabek Z. Simple learning-based robust nonlinear control of an electric pump for liquid-propellant rocket engines. Electronics. 2023;**12**:3527

[16] Mehndiratta M, Kayacan E, Reyhanoglu M, Kayacan E. Robust tracking control of aerial robots via a simple learning strategy-based feedback linearization. IEEE Access. 2019;**8**:1653-1669

[17] Reyhanoglu M, Jafari M, Rehan M. Simple learning-based robust trajectory tracking control of a 2-DOF helicopter system. Electronics. 2022;**11**:2075

[18] Perez-Grau FJ, Ragel R, Caballero F, Viguria A, Ollero A. An architecture for robust UAV navigation in GPS-denied areas. Journal of Field Robotics. 2018;**35**(1):121-145

Chapter 2

A Learning-Enhanced Robust Control Framework for Feedback Linearizable Autonomous Systems

Mohammad Jafari and Mahmut Reyhanoglu

Abstract

This chapter presents a learning-enhanced robust control framework for a broad class of nonlinear autonomous systems whose dynamics can be expressed in a feedback linearizable form. The core idea is to enhance classical feedback linearization with adaptive mechanisms that compensate for unknown disturbances and model uncertainties without requiring persistent excitation or detailed disturbance models. The method is grounded in nonlinear control theory and uses gradient descent learning rules to continuously adapt control parameters and disturbance estimates. The resulting closed-loop system achieves robust trajectory tracking while maintaining simplicity and interpretability in both implementation and analysis.

Keywords: robust control, nonlinear control, machine learning, robotics, autonomous systems

1. Introduction

Nonlinear autonomous systems are prevalent in various engineering domains, including robotics, aerospace, and automotive systems. A significant subset of these systems can be represented in a feedback linearizable form, allowing the application of linear control techniques to inherently nonlinear dynamics [1, 2]. Feedback linearization technique is employed to transform nonlinear system dynamics into an equivalent linear system through state and input transformations, facilitating the design of controllers that leverage the well-established linear control theory [3].

Despite the advantages offered by feedback linearization, real-world applications often involve challenges such as model uncertainties and unknown external disturbances. These uncertainties can degrade the performance of controllers designed under nominal conditions [4]. To address these issues, various control strategies have been developed. Classical robust control methods, such as sliding mode control, offer robustness against certain types of uncertainties but may introduce chattering and require precise knowledge of system bounds [5]. Adaptive control techniques adjust controller parameters in real-time to accommodate system variations, yet they often rely on persistent excitation conditions for parameter convergence [6].

In recent years, learning-based control approaches have gained prominence due to their ability to handle complex, uncertain environments [7–11]. Methods employing

Gaussian Processes (GPs) have been utilized to model and compensate for unknown disturbances in feedback linearizable systems, providing probabilistic guarantees and uncertainty quantification [7]. Reinforcement learning techniques have also been explored to learn optimal control policies without explicit system models, offering flexibility in handling a wide range of uncertainties [8–10]. Additionally, deep learning methods have been applied to approximate the feedback linearization transformations themselves, enabling control of systems with unknown dynamics [11].

While these advanced methods demonstrate impressive capabilities, they often come with increased computational complexity and reduced interpretability, posing challenges for practical implementation and analysis. In contrast, the approach presented in this chapter [12–15] aims to integrate the robustness of learning-based methods with the simplicity and clarity of classical control techniques. By enhancing feedback linearization with adaptive mechanisms grounded in gradient descent learning rules, the proposed framework compensates for unknown disturbances and model uncertainties without requiring persistent excitation or detailed disturbance models. This balance ensures robust trajectory tracking while maintaining ease of implementation and analytical tractability.

2. System modeling

We consider a class of second-order nonlinear autonomous systems with state vector $x = \left[x_1^T, x_2^T\right]^T \in \mathbb{R}^{2n}$, where $x_1 \in \mathbb{R}^n$ and $x_2 \in \mathbb{R}^n$ represent the generalized position and velocity, respectively. The system dynamics are described by:

$$\dot{x}_1 = x_2 \tag{1}$$

$$\dot{x}_2 = f(x) + g(x)u + d(x,t) \tag{2}$$

where:

- $f(x) : \mathbb{R}^{2n} \to \mathbb{R}^n$ is a smooth drift function capturing the nominal system dynamics.
- $g(x) : \mathbb{R}^{2n} \to \mathbb{R}^{n\times n}$ is a full-rank control effectiveness matrix.
- $u \in \mathbb{R}^n$ is the control input.
- $d(x,t) \in \mathbb{R}^n$ represents unknown bounded disturbances, including unmodeled dynamics and external inputs.

2.1 Assumptions

The following assumptions are made to facilitate control design and stability analysis:

Assumption 1 *Smoothness and Boundedness:*

$f(x)$, $g(x)$, $d(x, t)$ are continuously differentiable with bounded partial derivatives in the region of interest $X \subset \mathbb{R}^{2n}$.

Assumption 2 *Full-Rank Input Matrix:*

$g(x)$ is invertible for all $x \in X \subset \mathbb{R}^{2n}$; i.e., $\exists g^{-1}(x)$, for all $x \in X \subset \mathbb{R}^{2n}$.

Assumption 3 *Bounded Disturbances:*

$d(x, t)$ is bounded: $\|d(x,t)\| \leq \overline{d}$, and the time derivative $\dot{d}(x,t)$ is either bounded or slowly varying.

Assumption 4 *Tracking Reference:*

A twice-differentiable reference trajectory $r(t) = \left[r_1(t)^T, r_2(t)^T\right]^T = \left[r_1(t)^T, \dot{r}_1(t)^T\right]^T \in \mathbb{R}^{2n}$ *is provided, with* $\ddot{r}_1(t)$ *known.*

3. Control design

To achieve trajectory tracking, define the tracking error $e(t) = \begin{bmatrix} e_1(t) \\ e_2(t) \end{bmatrix} = \begin{bmatrix} r_1(t) - x_1(t) \\ r_2(t) - x_2(t) \end{bmatrix}$

Our goal is to design a control input u such that $e(t) \to 0$ as $t \to \infty$, despite the presence of $d(x, t)$. We propose a control law inspired by feedback linearization and disturbance estimation:

$$u = g^{-1}(x)\left(-f(x) + K_1 e_1 + K_2 e_2 + \ddot{r}_1 - \hat{d}\right) \tag{3}$$

where:

- $K_1, K_2 \in \mathbb{R}^{n \times n}$ are symmetric, positive definite gain matrices.
- $\hat{d}(t) \in \mathbb{R}^n$ is an estimate of the disturbance $d(x, t)$.

For simplicity, we will let $K_i = k_i I_n, \ \ k_i > 0, \ \ i = 1, 2$. Here I_n denotes the $n \times n$ identity matrix. Substituting the control input into the system yields the closed-loop error dynamics:

$$\dot{e}_1 = e_2 \tag{4}$$

$$\dot{e}_2 = -k_1 e_1 - k_2 e_2 + d - \hat{d} \tag{5}$$

3.1 Online update laws

Define a composite error metric:

$$c(e, k_d) = \dot{e}_2 + k_{2d} e_2 + k_{1d} e_1 \tag{6}$$

We minimize the cost function:

$$C = \frac{1}{2} c^T c \tag{7}$$

Using gradient descent, the gain updates and disturbance estimate update are:

$$\dot{k}_i = \alpha_i c^T e_i, \quad i = 1, 2 \tag{8}$$

$$\dot{\hat{d}} = -\alpha_{\hat{d}} c \tag{9}$$

where $\alpha_i, \alpha_{\hat{d}} > 0$ are learning rates.

3.2 Stability analysis

Assuming $\dot{d}\approx 0$ (slowly varying disturbance), we differentiate the second error equation:

$$\dddot{e}_1 + k_2\ddot{e}_1 + \left(k_1 + \dot{k}_2\right)\dot{e}_1 + \dot{k}_1 e_1 - \dot{\hat{d}} = 0 \tag{10}$$

Substituting $\dot{k}_i, \dot{\hat{d}}$ yields:

$$\dddot{e}_1 + k_2\ddot{e}_1 + k_1\dot{e}_1 + \left(\alpha_1 c^T e_1\right)e_1 + \left(\alpha_2 c^T \dot{e}_1\right)\dot{e}_1 + \alpha_{\hat{d}} c = 0 \tag{11}$$

Using the fact that $c = \ddot{e}_1 + k_{2d}\dot{e}_1 + k_{1d}e_1$, we express this as:

$$\dddot{e}_1 + A_1(\xi)\ddot{e}_1 + A_2(\xi)\dot{e}_1 + A_3(\xi)e_1 = 0 \tag{12}$$

where $\xi = \left[e_1^T, \dot{e}_1^T, \ddot{e}_1^T\right]^T$ and each $A_i(\xi) \in \mathbb{R}^{n\times n}$ is given by:

$$A_1 = \left(k_2 + \alpha_{\hat{d}}\right)I_n + \alpha_1 e_1 e_1^T + \alpha_2 \dot{e}_1 \dot{e}_1^T \tag{13}$$

$$A_2 = \left(k_1 + \alpha_{\hat{d}} k_{2d}\right)I_n + k_{2d}\left(\alpha_1 e_1 e_1^T + \alpha_2 \dot{e}_1 \dot{e}_1^T\right) \tag{14}$$

$$A_3 = k_{1d}\left(\alpha_{\hat{d}} I_n + \alpha_1 e_1 e_1^T + \alpha_2 \dot{e}_1 \dot{e}_1^T\right) \tag{15}$$

Assuming all gain matrices and learning rates are chosen such that $A_i(\xi)\succ 0$, we evaluate the characteristic polynomial at equilibrium:

$$\left[s^3 + \left(k_2 + \alpha_{\hat{d}}\right)s^2 + \left(k_1 + \alpha_{\hat{d}} k_{2d}\right)s + k_{1d}\alpha_{\hat{d}}\right]I_n = 0 \tag{16}$$

3.2.1 Routh-Hurwitz stability condition

The roots of the characteristic equation will have negative real parts if:

$$\left(k_2 + \alpha_{\hat{d}}\right)\left(k_1 + \alpha_{\hat{d}} k_{2d}\right) > k_{1d}\alpha_{\hat{d}} \tag{17}$$

This inequality ensures all Routh-Hurwitz determinants are positive, thereby guaranteeing exponential convergence of tracking error under appropriate gain selection.

3.3 Robustness and practical implementation

The proposed framework offers several robustness benefits:

- *Model-free disturbance compensation*: No explicit disturbance model is needed.
- *Simplicity*: Gradient learning is intuitive and computationally lightweight.
- *Robust to unmodeled dynamics*: Both matched disturbances and structured model uncertainties are addressed.
- *No persistent excitation (PE)*: Unlike many adaptive control schemes, this method does not require PE conditions.

This makes the method suitable for real-time embedded control of autonomous vehicles, robotic manipulators, and systems with uncertain dynamics and sensor noise.

3.4 Remarks

This generalized framework is applicable to a wide range of control-affine-nonlinear systems, including mechanical, robotic, and electromechanical systems. The disturbance estimate learning rule can be extended with adaptive filters, neural networks, or sliding mode observers for improved robustness. The error convergence analysis assumes a bounded state and a sufficiently smooth reference trajectory. Lyapunov or Input-to-State Stability (ISS) methods may be applied to relax some assumptions and extend to time-varying or unmodeled dynamics.

4. Numerical simulation results

To assess the effectiveness and generalizability of the proposed learning-enhanced robust nonlinear control approach, four representative systems were simulated in reference tracking (including both time-varying and constant) tasks and under external disturbances. All simulations took place over a 100-second time horizon (or 100 time steps), with control performance evaluated in the presence of both time-varying and constant disturbances.

4.1 Control of a 2-DOF helicopter system

A helicopter model, designated as a 2-DOF Helicopter Testbed, is employed to assess tracking performance in both the pitch (ϕ) and yaw (ψ) directions. We focus on the 2-DOF Helicopter System model discussed in [12]. The dynamical model of the helicopter system can be expressed as:

$$\ddot{\theta} = \frac{1}{a_1}\left[K_{pp}V_p + K_{py}V_y + a_2\right] \tag{18}$$

$$\ddot{\psi} = \frac{1}{b_1}\left[K_{yp}V_p + K_{yy}V_y + b_2\right] \tag{19}$$

where

$$a_1 = J_p + ml_{cm}^2,\ \ a_2 = -mgl_{cm}\cos\theta - D_p\dot{\theta} - ml_{cm}\dot{\psi}^2\sin\theta\cos\theta \tag{20}$$

$$b_1 = J_y + ml_{cm}^2\cos^2\theta,\ \ b_2 = -D_y\dot{\psi} + 2ml_{cm}^2\dot{\psi}\dot{\theta}\sin\theta\cos\theta \tag{21}$$

Here, m denotes the mass of the helicopter, and l_{cm} the distance from the axis of rotation to the center of mass. (D_p, D_y) represent viscous friction coefficients, $(K_{pp}, K_{py}, K_{yp}, K_{yy})$ denote the thrust torque constants, and J_p and J_y are the moments of inertia (MOIs) around the pitch and yaw axes, respectively. The control inputs to the DC torque motors are the voltages V_p and V_y, which actuate the pitch and yaw propellers, respectively. These voltages are constrained within the range [−24, 24] volts.

Now, define the following input transformation from (V_p, V_y) to (u_1, u_2):

$$\begin{bmatrix} u_1 \\ u_2 \end{bmatrix} = \begin{bmatrix} K_{pp} & K_{py} \\ K_{yp} & K_{yy} \end{bmatrix} \begin{bmatrix} V_p \\ V_y \end{bmatrix} \tag{22}$$

so that the above equations can be rewritten as

$$\ddot{\theta} = \frac{1}{a_1}(u_1 + a_2) \tag{23}$$

$$\ddot{\psi} = \frac{1}{b_1}(u_2 + b_2) \tag{24}$$

It is clear that each of these equations can be expressed as:

$$\dot{x}_1 = x_2 \tag{25}$$

$$\dot{x}_2 = f(x) + g(x)u + d \tag{26}$$

where $x = [x_1, x_2]^T \in \mathbb{R}^2$ and $u \in \mathbb{R}$ represent the state vector and control input, respectively. The external disturbances and modeling uncertainties are lumped as disturbance $d \in \mathbb{R}$, which is assumed bounded.

The desired reference trajectories were established as follows:

$$\phi_d(t) = 20\cos\left(\frac{t}{2}\right) \quad [\text{deg}], \quad \psi_d(t) = 45\sin\left(\frac{t}{4}\right) \quad [\text{deg}].$$

To evaluate the controllers' robustness, constant external torques of $0.5\ \text{N}\cdot\text{m}$ were applied as disturbances in both the pitch and yaw axes. The results indicated precise trajectory tracking and effective disturbance rejection. The simulation results for the closed-loop system are illustrated in **Figures 1** and **2**.

Figure 1 illustrates the time evolution of the pitch (ϕ) and yaw (ψ) under closed-loop controller operation, while **Figure 2** presents the commanded control signals.

During the closed-loop operation, the control actuation remains within acceptable limits. The results clearly demonstrate the effectiveness of the developed robust nonlinear control law in guiding the states to accurately track the reference trajectories.

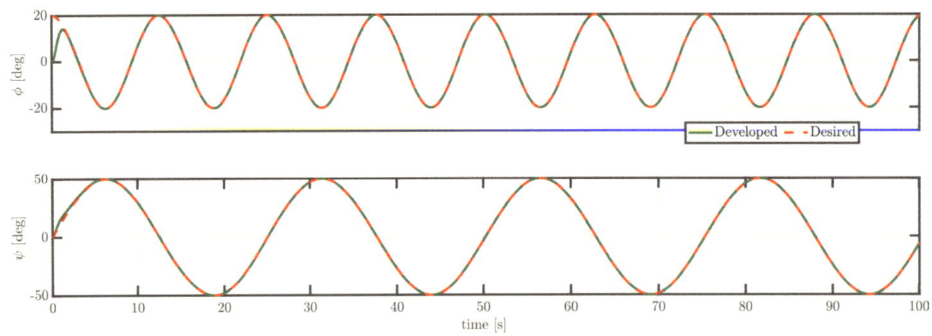

Figure 1.
Response of the pitch (ϕ) and yaw (ψ) (Closed-loop) for Case 1 (see Section 4.1).

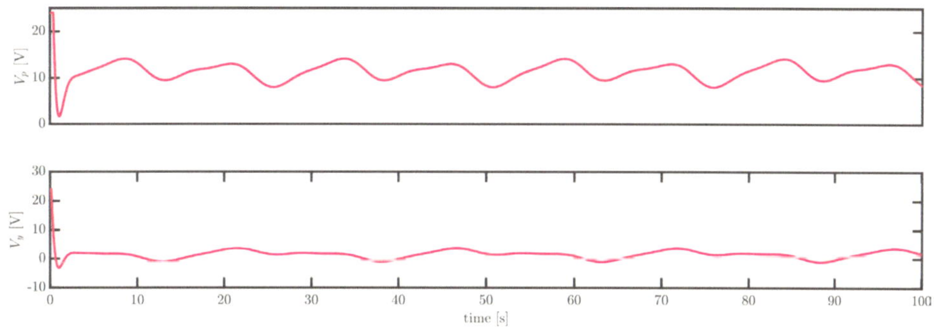

Figure 2.
Control inputs V_p and V_y for Case 1 (see Section 4.1).

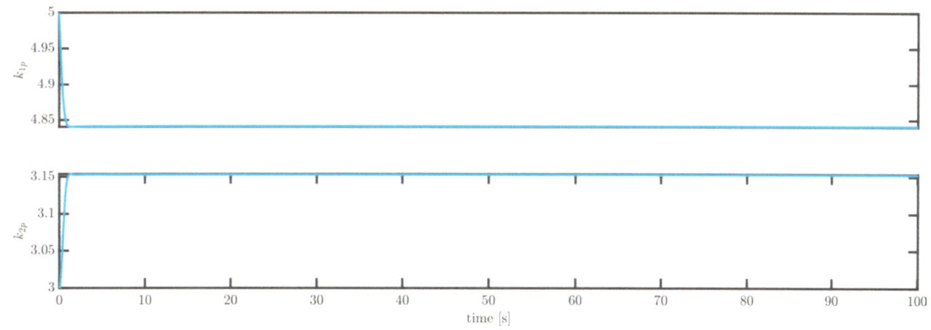

Figure 3.
k_{1p} and k_{2p} for Case 1 (see Section 4.1).

The calculated control gains (i.e., $k_{1(p,y)}$ and $k_{2(p,y)}$) along with the estimated disturbances (i.e., $\hat{d}_1$ and $\hat{d}_2$) for the controlled system are depicted in **Figures 3–5**, respectively. **Figure 3** shows that both control gains $k_{1(p,y)}$ and $k_{2(p,y)}$ converge to stable values, resulting in a well-regulated controlled system. Additionally, **Figure 5** illustrates that the estimated disturbances are effectively compensated, highlighting the nonlinear controller's capability to estimate and mitigate these disturbances.

4.2 Control of a PPR manipulator

A planar PPR (Prismatic-Prismatic-Revolute) robotic manipulator is simulated to follow a dynamic trajectory in Cartesian space. We focus on the PPR manipulator model discussed in [13]. Consider a planar PPR robot consisting of three joints—two prismatic and one revolute—operating on a horizontal plane, allowing gravitational potential energy to be neglected. The Cartesian coordinates of the revolute joint are denoted by (x, y), and the orientation of the third link is represented by θ. The control inputs for the system are the torque τ applied at the revolute joint and the forces F_x and F_y actuating the two prismatic joints. The physical parameters for the PPR robot include the mass of the three links m_1, m_2, m_3; the distance l from the revolute joint to the center of mass (CoM) of the third link; and the moment of inertia J_3 of the third link about its CoM. The dynamical model can be obtained by using Lagrangian formulation as follows:

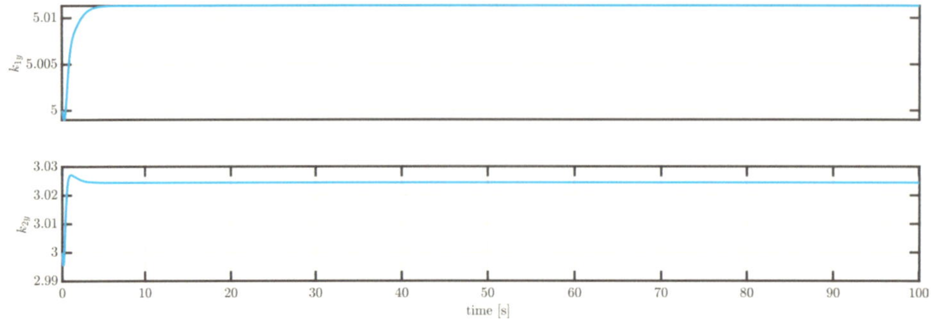

Figure 4.
k_{1y} and k_{2y} for Case 1 (see Section 4.1).

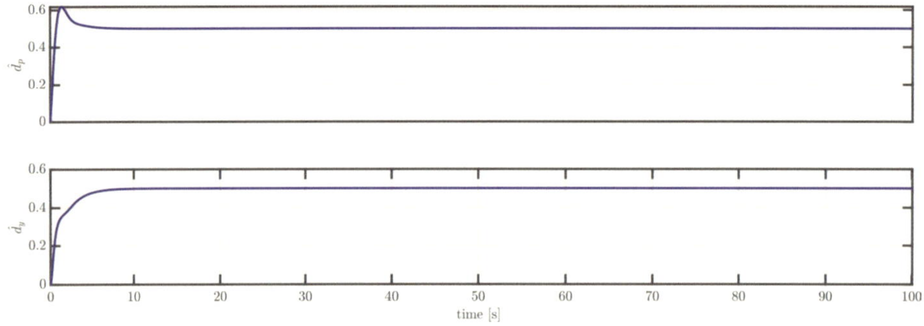

Figure 5.
$\hat{d}_1$ and $\hat{d}_2$ for Case 1 (see Section 4.1).

$$m_x\ddot{x} - m_3 l\ddot{\theta}\sin\theta - m_3 l\dot{\theta}^2\cos\theta = F_x \tag{27}$$

$$m_y\ddot{y} + m_3 l\ddot{\theta}\cos\theta - m_3 l\dot{\theta}^2\sin\theta = F_y \tag{28}$$

$$J\ddot{\theta} + m_3 l(\ddot{y}\cos\theta - \ddot{x}\sin\theta) = \tau \tag{29}$$

where $m_x = m_1 + m_2 + m_3$, $m_y = m_2 + m_3$ and $J = J_3 + m_3 l^2$.

Define by $x = \left[x_1^T, x_2^T\right]^T = \left[q^T, \dot{q}^T\right]^T$ the state. Then Eqs. (27)–(29) can be expressed in state space form as

$$\dot{x}_1 = x_2 \tag{30}$$

$$\dot{x}_2 = f(x) + g(x_1)u + d \tag{31}$$

where

$$f(x) = -M^{-1}(x_1)F(x),\ g(x_1) = M^{-1}(x_1)B(x_1),\ d = M^{-1}[\Delta(x) + w] \tag{32}$$

where d represents a lumped disturbance vector that comprises modeling uncertainties and external disturbances.

The desired reference trajectories were defined as:

$$x_d(t) = \cos(t) \quad [\mathrm{m}], \quad y_d(t) = \sin(t/4) \quad [\mathrm{m}], \quad \theta_d(t) = 45\cos(t/4) \quad [\mathrm{deg}].$$

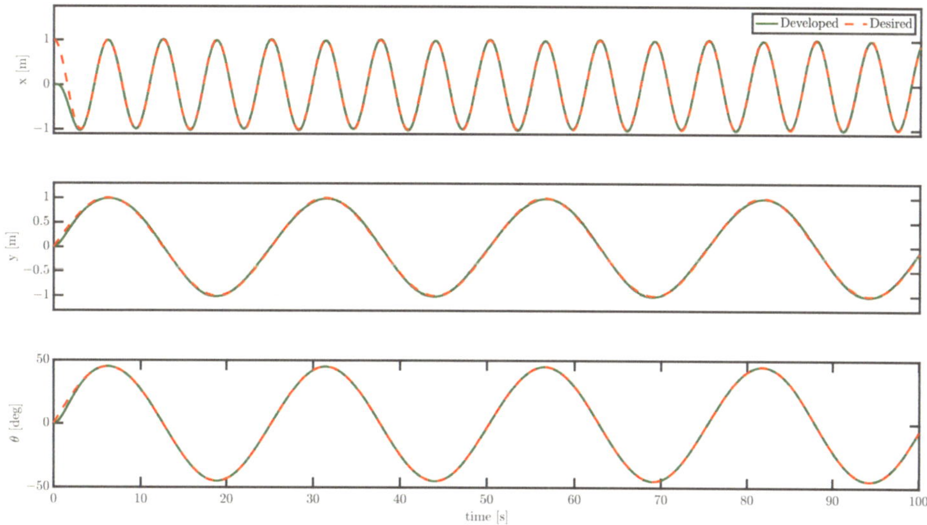

Figure 6.
Response of x, y, *and* θ *(Closed-loop) for Case* 2 *(see Section 4.2).*

Time-varying external disturbances were applied to each joint, with translational disturbances represented as $d_x(t) = d_y(t) = 0.5\cos(t/2)\,\mathrm{m/s^2}$, and the rotational disturbance given by $d_\theta(t) = 0.5\cos(t/2)\,\mathrm{rad/s^2}$. The controller effectively maintained tracking performance despite these input perturbations. The results of the closed-loop simulation are illustrated in **Figures 6** and 7.

Figure 6 illustrates the time evolution of x, y, and θ under the operation of a closed-loop controller, while **Figure 7** showcases the commanded control signals.

During the closed-loop operation, the control actuation remains within acceptable limits. The results clearly highlight the effectiveness of the developed robust nonlinear control law in guiding the states to accurately track the reference trajectories.

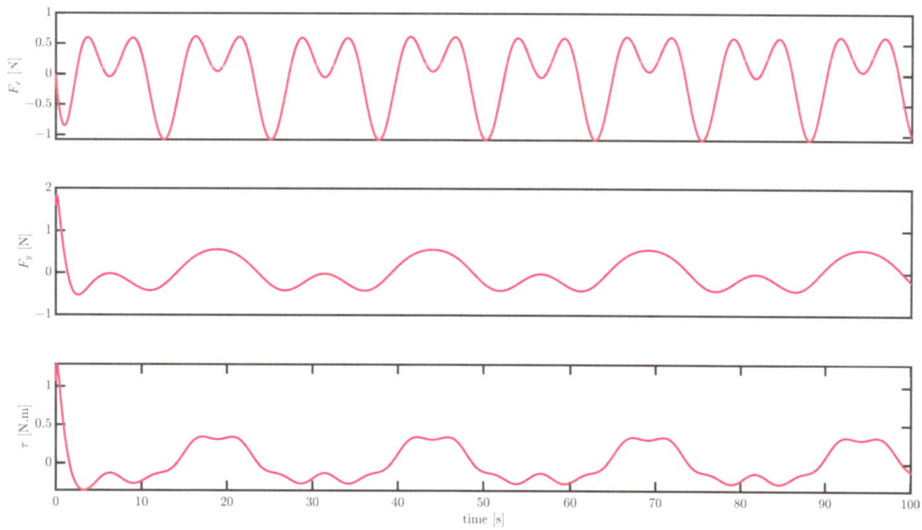

Figure 7.
Control inputs F_x, F_y, *and* τ *for Case* 2 *(see Section 4.2).*

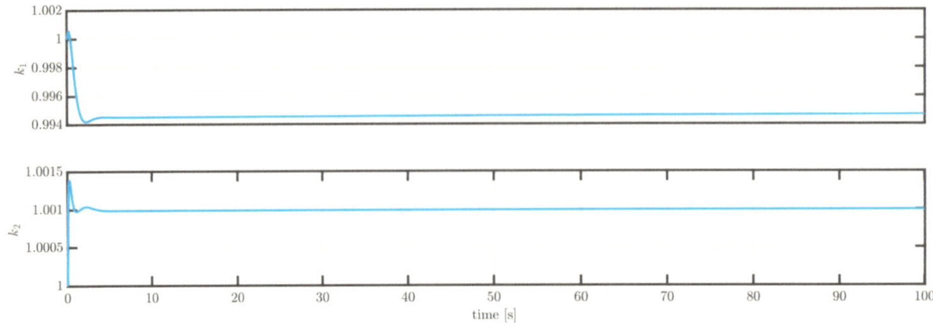

Figure 8.
k_1 and k_2 for Case 2 (see Section 4.2).

The computed control gains (i.e., k_1 and k_2), along with the estimated disturbances (i.e., $\hat{d}_x, \hat{d}_y$, and $\hat{d}_\theta$) for the controlled system, are depicted in **Figures 8** and **9**, respectively. **Figure 8** shows that both control gains k_1 and k_2 converge to specific values, resulting in a stable controlled system. Additionally, **Figure 9** illustrates the effective compensation of the estimated disturbances, underscoring the nonlinear controller's ability to estimate and mitigate these disturbances.

4.3 Control of electric pumps for liquid-propellant rocket engines

To assess the controller in a propulsion context, we regulate the mass flow rate of an electric pump in a liquid-propellant rocket engine utilizing a piecewise time-varying reference signal. We refer to the Electric Pump for Liquid-Propellant Rocket Engines model discussed in [14]. The following equations describe the electric pump dynamics:

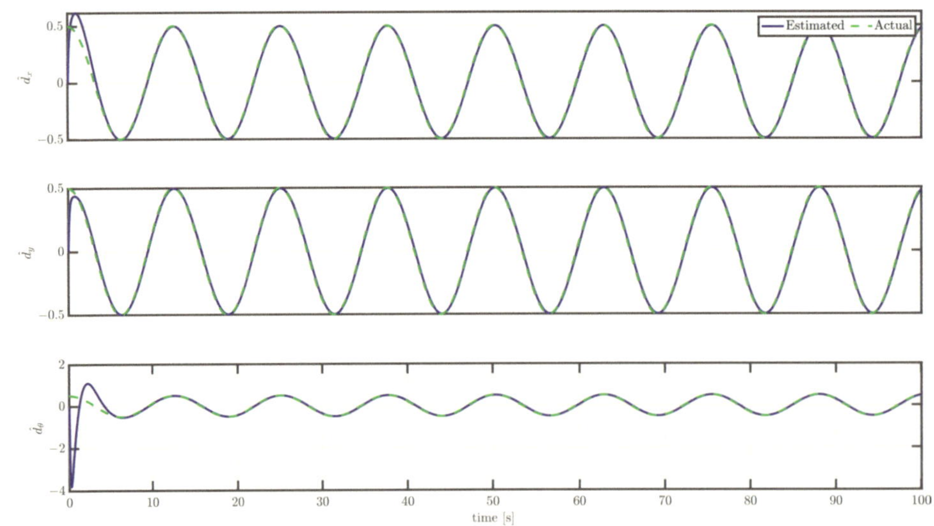

Figure 9.
$\hat{d}_x, \hat{d}_y$, and $\hat{d}_\theta$ for Case 2 (see Section 4.2).

$$\frac{dI_a}{dt} = -\frac{R_a}{L_a}I_a - \frac{\gamma_r k_v}{L_a}\dot{m} + \frac{1}{L_a}V_a \tag{33}$$

$$\frac{d\dot{m}}{dt} = \frac{k_t}{\gamma_r J_m}I_a - \frac{B_m}{J_m}\dot{m} - \frac{900k\gamma_r}{\pi^2 J_m}\dot{m}^2 \tag{34}$$

where (V_a, I_a) denote the armature voltage and the armature current, (R_a, L_a) are the armature resistance and inductance, $\dot{m}$ is the mass flow rate, k_v is the motor voltage constant, γ_r and k are physical constants, and J_m and B_m are the motor moment of inertia and viscous friction coefficient, respectively.

Selecting $u = V_a$ as the control input, $y = \dot{m}$ as the output, and $x = [x_1, x_2]^T = [y, \dot{y}]^T \in \mathbb{R}^2$ as the state vector, the mathematical model can be expressed as

$$\dot{x}_1 = x_2 \tag{35}$$

$$\dot{x}_2 = f(x) + bu + d \tag{36}$$

where

$$f(x) = -a_2 x_1 - a_1 x_2 - c_1 x_1^2 - c_2 x_1 x_2 \tag{37}$$

and $d \in \mathbb{R}$ (assumed bounded) represents the modeling uncertainties and external disturbances. Here

$$a_1 = \frac{R_a}{L_a} + \frac{B_m}{J_m}, \quad a_2 = \frac{R_a B_m}{L_a J_m} + \frac{k_t k_v}{L_a J_m} \tag{38}$$

$$c_1 = \frac{900k\gamma_r R_a}{\pi^2 L_a J_m}, \quad c_2 = \frac{1800k\gamma_r}{\pi^2 J_m}, \quad b = \frac{k_t}{\gamma_r L_a J_m} \tag{39}$$

The desired reference trajectory $\dot{m}_d(t)$ is defined as follows:

$$\dot{m}_d(t) = \begin{cases} 0.05t, & 0 \le t < 10, \\ 0.5 - 0.05(t-10), & 10 \le t < 20, \\ 0.05(t-20), & 20 \le t < 30, \\ 0.5 - 0.05(t-30), & 30 \le t < 40, \\ 0.05(t-40), & 40 \le t < 50, \\ 0.5 - 0.05(t-50), & 50 \le t < 60, \\ 0.05(t-60), & 60 \le t < 70, \\ 0.5 - 0.05(t-70), & 70 \le t < 80, \\ 0.05(t-80), & 80 \le t < 90, \\ 0.5 - 0.05(t-90), & t \ge 90. \end{cases}$$

This pattern reflects the operational variations common in pump flow profiles during real-world missions. The proposed control strategy demonstrated smooth tracking and resilience to parameter uncertainties. The results of the closed-loop simulation are illustrated in **Figures 10** and **11**.

Figure 10 illustrates the time evolution of the mass flow rate $(\dot{m})$ under the operation of the closed-loop controller, while **Figure 11** showcases the commanded control signal.

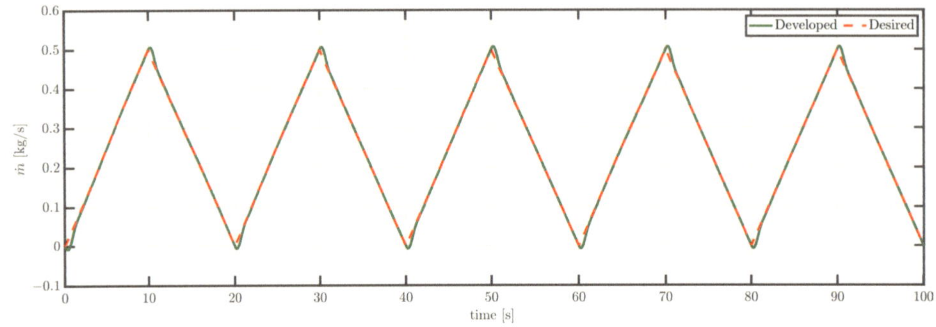

Figure 10.
Response of $\dot{m}$ (Closed-loop) for Case 3 (see Section 4.3).

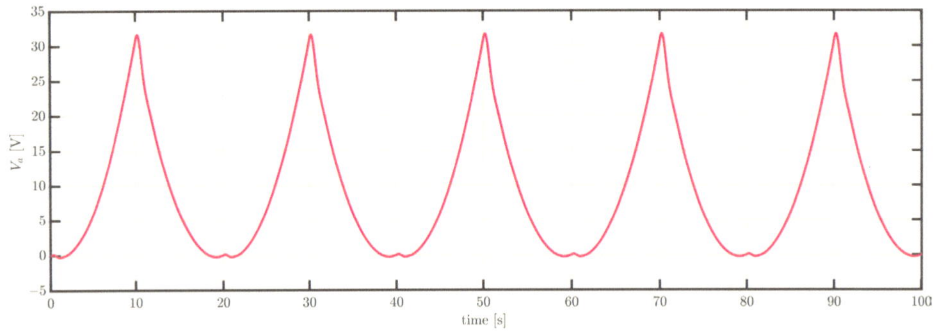

Figure 11.
Control input V_a for Case 3 (see Section 4.3).

During the closed-loop operation, the control actuation remains within acceptable limits. The results clearly demonstrate the efficacy of the proposed robust nonlinear control law in guiding the system state to accurately track the reference trajectory.

The calculated control gains (i.e., k_1 and k_2), along with the estimated disturbances (i.e., $\hat{d}$), for the controlled system are presented in **Figures 12** and **13**, respectively. **Figure 12** shows that both control gains k_1 and k_2 converge to specific values, resulting in a stable controlled system. Meanwhile, **Figure 13** illustrates the effective compensation of estimated disturbances, underscoring the nonlinear controller's ability to estimate and mitigate these disturbances.

4.4 Control of thermoacoustic oscillations

To illustrate scalability to higher-order distributed parameter systems, the proposed controller is implemented to mitigate thermoacoustic instabilities. We consider the Thermoacoustic Oscillation System model discussed in [15]. The dynamical model for the thermoacoustic duct's natural modes can be expressed as:

$$M\ddot{\eta} + C\dot{\eta} + G\eta + w(t) = Bu, \tag{40}$$

where $B,\ C,\ G \in \mathbb{R}^{N\times N}$ are constant matrices and $w(t)$ represents a lumped disturbance vector that comprises modeling uncertainties and external disturbances. Define

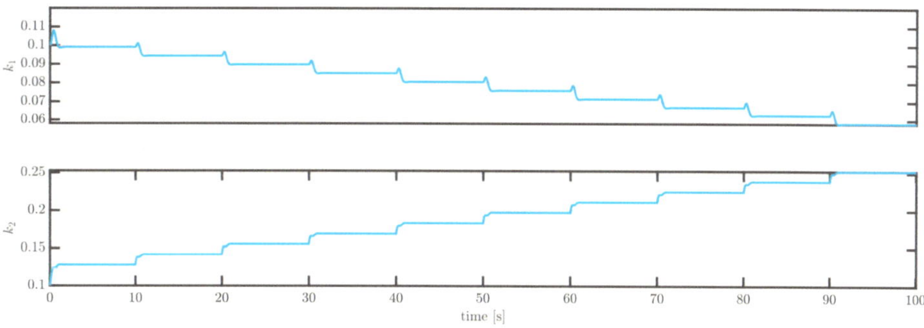

Figure 12.
k_1 and k_2 for Case 3 (see Section 4.3).

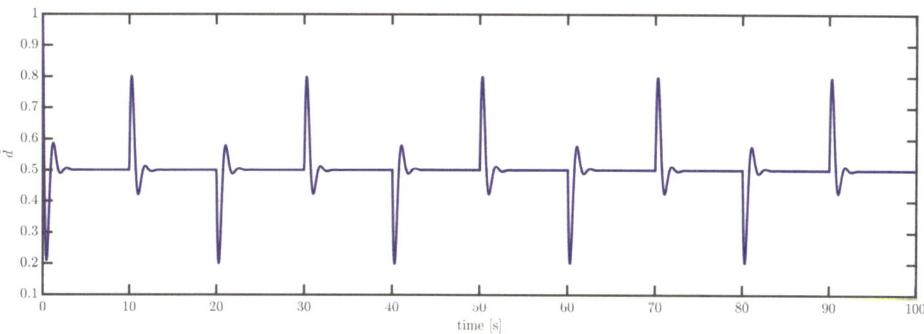

Figure 13.
$\hat{d}$ for Case 3 (see Section 4.3).

the state vector as $x = \left[x_1^T, x_2^T\right]^T = \left[\eta^T, \dot{\eta}^T\right]^T$. Under this formulation, the equation presented in (40) can be reformulated into a state space representation as

$$\dot{x}_1 = x_2, \tag{41}$$

$$\dot{x}_2 = f(x) + g(x)u + d(t), \tag{42}$$

where

$$f(x) = -M^{-1}(Gx_1 + Cx_2), \;\; g(x) = M^{-1}B, \;\; d(t) = -M^{-1}w(t). \tag{43}$$

We consider a thermoacoustic system comprising four modes (N = 4) and four actuators (K = 4). This setup simulates a realistic scenario in combustion chambers, where multiple dominant modes interact and need to be controlled simultaneously. Simulation results affirmed the controllers' efficacy in reducing oscillations while effectively managing complex mode-actuator couplings. The outcomes of the closed-loop simulation are presented in **Figures 14** and **15**.

Figure 14 illustrates the time evolution of the modes η_1, η_2, η_3, and η_4 under the operation of the closed-loop controller, while **Figure 15** presents the commanded control signals.

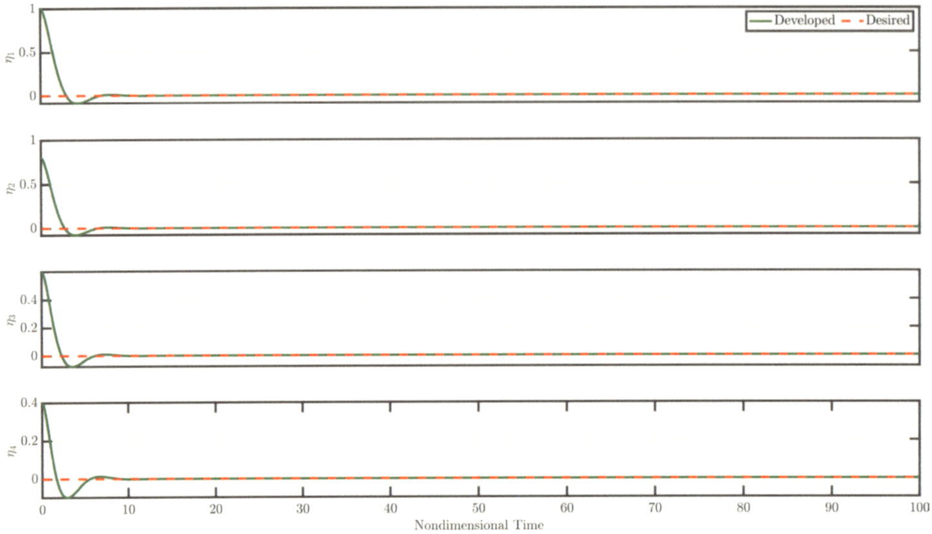

Figure 14.
Response of $\eta_1, \eta_2, \eta_3,$ and η_4 (Closed-loop) for Case 4 (see Section 4.4).

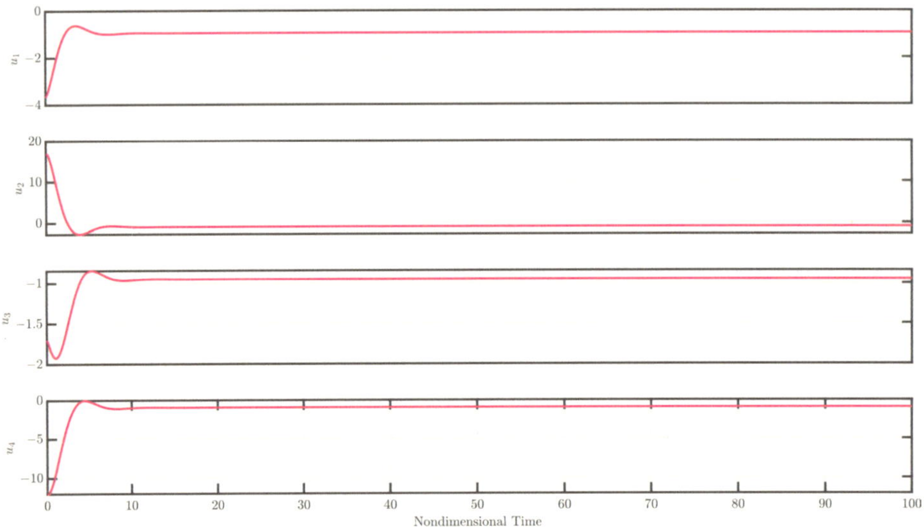

Figure 15.
Control inputs $u_1, u_2, u_3,$ and u_4 for Case 4 (see Section 4.4).

Throughout the closed-loop operation, the control actuation remains within acceptable limits. The results clearly highlight the effectiveness of the proposed robust nonlinear control law in driving the states to zero.

The calculated control gains (i.e., k_1 and k_2) and the estimated disturbances (i.e., $\hat{d}_1, \hat{d}_2, \hat{d}_3,$ and $\hat{d}_4$) for the controlled system are depicted in **Figures 16** and **17**, respectively. **Figure 16** shows that both control gains k_1 and k_2 converge to specific values, resulting in a stable controlled system. Meanwhile, **Figure 17** illustrates that the estimated disturbances are effectively compensated, showcasing the nonlinear controller's ability to estimate and mitigate these disturbances.

DOI: http://dx.doi.org/10.5772/intechopen.1011723

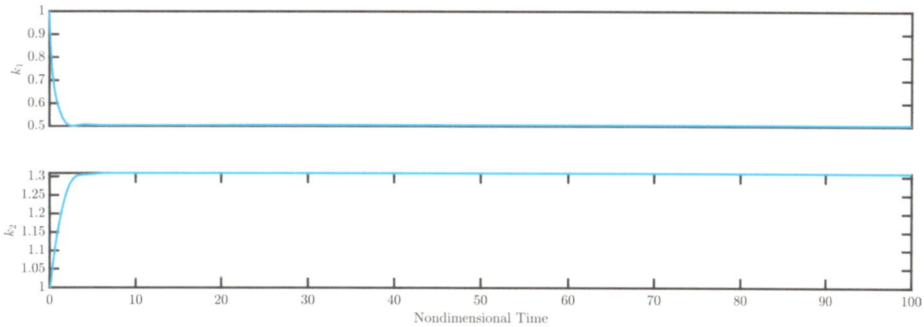

Figure 16.
k_1 and k_2 for Case 4 (see Section 4.4).

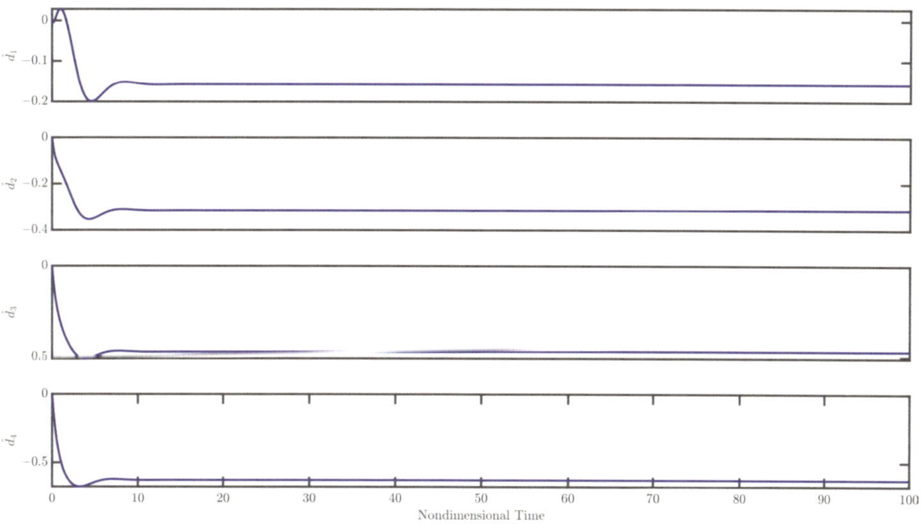

Figure 17.
$\hat{d}_1, \hat{d}_2, \hat{d}_3$, and $\hat{d}_4$ for Case 4 (see Section 4.4).

5. Conclusion

We have presented a unified learning-based robust control framework for feedback linearizable systems. The approach ensures trajectory tracking in the presence of disturbances and uncertainties through adaptive disturbance estimation and optional gain tuning. Four examples have been considered: control of a 2-DOF helicopter system, control of a PPR manipulator, control of an electric pump for liquid-propellant rocket engines, and control of thermoacoustic oscillations. Future work includes experimental validation and extension to underactuated and non-feedback linearizable systems.

Author details

Mohammad Jafari[1] and Mahmut Reyhanoglu[2*]

1 Robotics Engineering Program, Columbus State University, USA

2 School of Engineering, Wentworth Institute of Technology, USA

*Address all correspondence to: mreyhanoglu@icloud.com

References

[1] Isidori A. Nonlinear Control Systems: An Introduction. Berlin-Heidelberg: Springer; 1985

[2] Slotine J-JE, Li W, et al. Applied Nonlinear Control, Vol. 199. NJ: Prentice Hall Englewood Cliffs; 1991

[3] Khalil HK, Grizzle JW. Nonlinear Systems, Volume 3. Saddle River, NJ: Prentice hall Upper; 2002

[4] Zhou K, Doyle JC, Glover K. Robust and Optimal Control. New York: Prentice-Hall, Inc.; 1996

[5] Utkin V, I. Sliding Modes in Control and Optimization. Springer Science & Business Media; 2013

[6] Ioannou PA, Sun J. Robust adaptive control, volume 1. Saddle River, NJ: PTR Prentice-Hall Upper; 1996

[7] Berkenkamp F, Turchetta M, Schoellig A, Krause A. Safe model-based reinforcement learning with stability guarantees. Advances in Neural Information Processing Systems. 2017; **30**:1-11

[8] Kiumarsi B, Vamvoudakis KG, Modares H, Lewis FL. Optimal and autonomous control using reinforcement learning: A survey. IEEE Transactions on Neural Networks and Learning Systems. 2017;**29**(6):2042-2062

[9] Westenbroek T, Fridovich-Keil D, Mazumdar E, Arora S, Valmik Prabhu S, Sastry S, et al. Feedback linearization for uncertain systems via reinforcement learning. In: 2020 IEEE International Conference on Robotics and Automation (ICRA). IEEE; 2020. pp. 1364-1371

[10] Hajiahmadi F, Jafari M, Reyhanoglu M. Machine learning-based control of autonomous vehicles for solar panel cleaning systems in agricultural solar farms. AgriEngineering. 2024;**6**(2): 1417-1435

[11] Goswami R, G, Krishnamurthy P, Khorrami F. Data-driven deep learning based feedback linearization of systems with unknown dynamics. In: 2023 American Control Conference (ACC). San Diego, California, USA: IEEE; 2023. pp. 66-71

[12] Reyhanoglu M, Jafari M, Rehan M. Simple learning-based robust trajectory tracking control of a 2-dof helicopter system. Electronics. 2022;**11**(13):2075

[13] Reyhanoglu M, Jafari M. A simple learning approach for robust tracking control of a class of dynamical systems. Electronics. 2023;**12**(9):2026

[14] Jafari M, Reyhanoglu M, Kozhabek Z. Simple learning-based robust nonlinear control of an electric pump for liquid-propellant rocket engines. Electronics. 2023;**12**(16):3527

[15] Reyhanoglu M, Jafari M. Learning-enabled robust control of thermoacoustic oscillations. Electronics. 2025;**14**(9):1771

Chapter 3

Augmented Radiation Tracking System for Autonomous Fixed Wing Platform with Model-Based Control and Inverse Dynamics and Path Following

Valentin Penev

Abstract

The demonstrator of a fixed-wing tandem unmanned aerial vehicle (UAV) is designed for the passive detection of radiation fixed on ground targets. When the target does not emit, the autonomous platform navigates to the target using a proposed navigation and guidance algorithm. A specific approach is used to design the 6D trajectory to the target. Novel combinations of a three-loop autopilot, inverse dynamics control, and model-based control are used to follow the platform's path to the target. The absence of a permanently radiated signal from the target poses challenges, which have been addressed in this research. Some challenges of the passive radiation tracking, autonomously flying platform, particularly inaccurate trajectory control, have, in certain instances, been avoidable. Until a certain point, the strapped-down radiation seeker passes the elevation and azimuth of the target to the autopilot. Then, the vehicle flies in full autonomous mode to the very close vicinity of the target, where the secondary seeker takes control. A solution in SimuliNK was developed to simulate vehicle dynamics, inertial sensors, and its Guidance Navigation and Control (GNC) algorithms. The proposed unconventional approach for determining platform attitude in 6D space enhances guidance accuracy. An original model-based control with specific tuning algorithms is proposed, evaluated, and tested in simulations and some real flights. The results show that the vehicle's performance in response to excessive and agile roll, pitch, and yaw is extremely sensitive to the quality of guidance. The proposed joint simulation model was almost unaffected by the lack of a radiation signal from the target and precisely followed the discretized positions and altitude, as well as the roll, pitch, and flight path angle of the 6D trajectory.

Keywords: fixed-wing UAV, AHRS, model-based control, inverse dynamics, flight simulation, tandem aircraft

1. Introduction

The Augmented Radiation Tracking Demonstrator (ARTSD) system is primarily designed to detect, track, and hit fixed ground radiating targets. The system resolves problems generated by situations where the target does not emit a permanent signal; therefore, the demonstrator should fly autonomously to the target along his own created trajectory. The ARTSD is a small-size fixed-wing platform, which is launched in a handheld manner. Introducing the improved system, equipped with a radiation seeker and a daylight or infrared camera, into the modern combat scenario will give an advanced ability to destroy targets more accurately without a permanent radiating cycle. The operating range is about 20 km, and the flight time is about an hour. After some loitering, the emitting target's attitude is identified with down-range elevation and down-range azimuth. The vehicle will fly autonomously to the target and do offensive or evasive maneuvers along the pre-calculated trajectory. Generally, the vehicle will not need operator input during flight to lock and terminate individual objects, but this will depend on each application. Autonomous platforms similar to ARTSD should deploy precision sensors (tactical grade) and guidance [1]. According to the initially predefined requirements, we used low-cost industrial-grade inertial sensors of AHRS [2–5] and attempted to achieve the best performance from them and the overall system.

The research reported here develops a high-fidelity flight model [4, 5] of the ARTSD vehicle. A guidance algorithm has been developed to imitate the flying styles of the actual system in the presence of a target radiation signal. Partial test flights of ARTSD have been conducted to verify the accuracy of the proposed model and guidance algorithms. The ARTSD is a fixed-wing tandem with two pFLCS and sFLCS, which fulfill closed-loop system requirements. It has also been demonstrated that the interaction between two strapped-down seekers, the aerodynamics of the vehicle, and flight control system (FLCS) is a significant factor in its response to damaging the target. In real life, many factors affect the detection and guidance of the target. Firstly, the platform undergoes environmental turbulence and oscillations generated by the airframe. Secondly, natural hurdles due to the environment such as fog, clouds, rain, or snow can affect the signal strength. All those features affect the performance of guidance.

A novel modification of model-based control and its algorithm for tuning [3–5] are proposed and tested in the simulation and real flights. The strapped-down seeker model passes the deflections along the ray array to the target to the autopilot. The time responses, which envisage the vehicle's performance in response to excessive and agile roll, pitch, and yaw, are extremely dependable to the quality of guidance. The goal of the proposed algorithm is to navigate the platform (in the absence of target radiation signal) to the closest possible vicinity to the target when the secondary visual or infra red (IR) seeker will be able to guide exactly to the target. The target may also use countermeasure techniques to affect the platform guidance.

Longitudinal autopilots for tactical missiles and precisely guided weapons have been successfully used for an extended period. The "classic" three-loop autopilot (often referred to as the "Raytheon autopilot" [6]) has been the design shape of many. The design objective of any autopilot is to use appropriately read sensor measures and AHRS calculations to produce a stable response that robustly follows command inputs and meets requirements. The classic three-loop autopilot uses the desired longitudinal and lateral acceleration as the command inputs. The measured feedback inputs are the detected acceleration, pitch rate, and pitch angle or flight path angle. This paper takes a closer look at several possible combinations between three-loop autopilots, model-based control [3], and invers invers dynamic control (IIDC) [2]. The feedback inputs to all topologies should be measured or estimated with high accuracy. MBC and its tuning procedure should replace the gain-scheduling procedure, which is almost mandatory in complex systems. The same applies to IIDC, which will calculate directly the required pitch or elevator fin command from longitudinal acceleration demand. Several three-loop autopilot topologies can be shown to be almost equivalent from a closed-loop system view. Potentially, two measures can be used to form the feedback: the acceleration (Azm), the pitch rate (qm), and the pitch (θp). The following integrals ∫Azmdt, ∫ qmdt, and ∫θp dt are also available. Usually, the integral part leads to overshooting, which is not appropriate in the current research. The integral part will be replaced by an appropriate model-based control. The compensator transfer function in the MBC velocity loop plays a significant role.

The article considers the design, performance, and augmented radiation tracking system control of the platform.

The requirements for aerodynamics are basically two:

- Very stable and smooth flight path angle behavior
- Ability to do stable and controllable steep dives.

The general requirements for flight control system are:

- Precise calculation of 6D path to the target, which will allow flying to the target without radiation signal
- Precise following of the predefined flight path, with minimal parallel motion along it
- The flight control system is supported by GPS.

1.1 Background

The system comprises two subsystems: a ground control unit (GCS) and an ARTSD vehicle. The ARTSD vehicle is launched by hand. The ARTSD vehicle airframe shown in **Figure 1** consists of two mid-body wings, a fuselage, and a rudder. The control surfaces are selected to be ailerons (front wing), elevators (aft wing), flaps (aft wing), and rudder. Using a minimal set of control surfaces, only elevons will not cause the loss of controllability and precision, except in the case of agile changes in roll, pitch, and yaw.

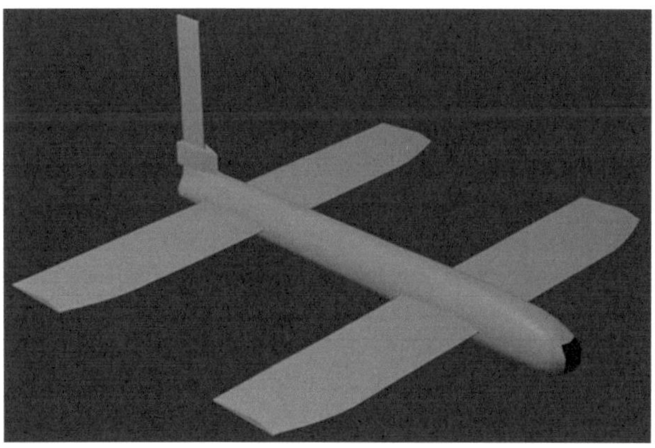

Figure 1.
The geometry of ARTSD.

Attitude Heading Reference System (AHRS) calculates the vehicle's orientation and gets some estimated parameters from Flight AeroDynamics (FAD). The Augmented Radiation Tracking System (ARTS), or strapped-down seekers module, consists of a passive radiation seeker and a visual tracking module. Both seekers have their processor, which process the data and feed the autopilot with demands in lateral and longitudinal channels and some additional information. The primary Flight Control System (pFLCS) generates control surface commands. The secondary FLCS is responsible for IIDC, FAD, FSS, and additional calculations to aid the AHRS. Guidance is based on a DoA vector and a 6D trajectory, calculated at a certain point when the target still emits a radio signal. That could happen several times during the flight to the target. Moreover, the seeker must have a limited role concerning the target to maintain a lock with it. That is why the "skid-to-turn" topology will be used. The main problem arises when the seeker maintains the direction of the target, but the guidance and aerodynamics respond poorly to it. The second failure happens when excessive and agile yaw, pitch, or roll causes seeker failure. The third badly behaved situation is AHRS's fidelity of attitude determination, which is of primary importance. The requirement for low-cost AHRS plays an important role. The proof of the proposed approaches is done by simulations, which include evaluation of the response of an ARTSD to both types of trajectories midcourse and terminal stage and estimate of the probability of failure in both cases. The flight of the autonomous platform [2, 3, 7] has four stages: Launch, Climb, Loitering (midcourse), and Terminal. The second phase of flight is the climb out. The ARTSD climbs constantly until it reaches a desired altitude of several thousand meters [8]. Then, the system starts searching for a decent emitting signal.

The following states are important to start the calculations:

- Earth coordinates X_e, Y_e, Z_e,
- body coordinates (u,w),
- pitch angle θ,
- pitch rate $q = \dot{\theta}$.

The following **Figure 2** summarizes the navigation geometry and the relationship between the inertial and body fixed frames, the flight path angle γ, the pitch angle θ, and the incidence angle α. A highly modified classic three-loop autopilot topology

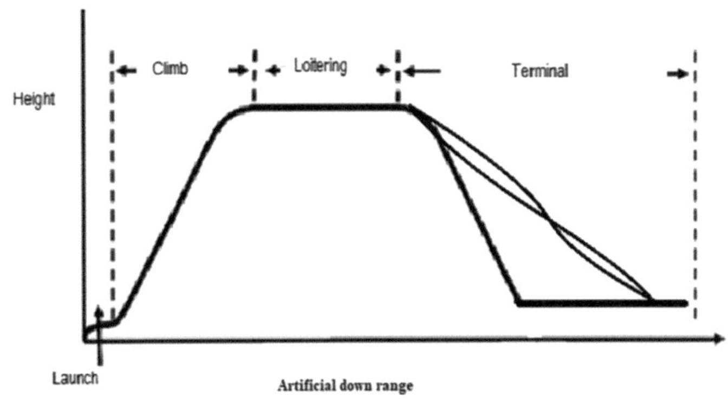

Figure 2.
Flight stages of the platform.

controls the flight path angle γ. This autopilot shapes the flight path angle by bringing adequate impulses of normal acceleration az. The average acceleration is produced by moving the elevator deflection δe and rarely flaps deflection δf to cause pitching and vary the amount of lift. Autopilot uses specific model-based control in the pitch rate loop q and the az and γ loops.

The airframe dynamics are nonlinear, and the aerodynamic forces and moments depend highly on speed V, altitude h, and angle of attack α. To obtain suitable performance throughout the α, V, β flight behavior, the autopilot gains must be shaped as a function of α, β, and V to compensate for changes in platform dynamics. This adjustment process is called "gain scheduling," and α, V, and β are the scheduling variables [4]. The autopilot gain scheduling is replaced by MBC, which has the same features when we do multiparameter tuning with some range for each parameter. If the sideslip angle is assumed to be minimal or zero, then in the Simulink model, gain schedules are implemented as look-up tables driven by measurements of α and V. MBC tuning procedure is a nonlinear technique for controlling nonlinear or time-varying plants, and it involves the following three significant steps:

- Calculate the controller gains for the nonlinear dynamics at each operating condition with a proposed full-scale search method.

- Settle the gain values to provide a smooth transition between operating conditions.

Here, steps 1 and 2 are combined by parameterizing the autopilot gains as first-order and second-order continuous-time systems and directly tuning the polynomial coefficients for the entire flight envelope. This approach secures smooth gain variations as a function of α and V.

1.2 Augmented radiation tracking system

The ARTSD can detect and recognize the targets by the operator's manual lock. The initial object detection and continuous-time tracking should be done in the visual tracking system or by the operator. That feature will be used in the final approach to the target. The visual tracking system has fallen out of interest in the current research; the FLCS should guide the platform as close as possible to the target, where the vision tracking system will be turned on. The process of automatically detecting, recognizing, and tracking objects is essential in determining specific criteria. The real-time and robust procedure is used to augment the accuracy of the demonstrator's arrival at the target. The ARTSD will give an additional extra feature to create a reliable way to fly very close to the target, which has already stopped emitting. The lock will be automatic, which means the passive radiation seeker has stable and reliable azimuth and elevation to the target. The manual lock is just an option. It will reduce the autonomy, and the system will not operate in silent mode, which is an important feature. That means the target is ill-defined or has been hit something because we do not have "another option."

A flying autonomous platform equipped with ARTSD will be able to function in the following way with the locked target:

- Seeking the target and locking it are done before following the final trajectory;

- Follow the 6D trajectory to the target;

- Do some offensive and defensive maneuvers, which are incorporated into 6D trajectory.

The visual tracking seeker is used in the very last stage. Dual Mode Seeker – Two heads are better than one.

The radiation seeker and vision tracking seeker are out of the scope of current research.

The control strategy is built on a complex trajectory (please see **Figure 3**) to the nearest target position and estimating platform position and attitude over time, as well as the guidance and control of the platform. This permits interactive compromises between seeker design and guidance and control system design to be evaluated during the precise simulation. A better approach is to use ΔN, ΔE, and ΔH or to create an artificial horizontal line as in **Figure 3**.

The performance of the anti-radiation seeker plays a vital role in modern intelligent munitions detection tasks [9]. However, in practice, the multi-path reflection, the active decoy jamming, and the multiple coherent and relevant sources might decrease the anti-radiation seeker's precise detection and estimation performance in estimating the target's Direction of Arrival (DoA). Currently, dual-mode seekers for ground-to-ground smart munitions have remained a valuable solution. One challenge in combining passive radiation and visual tracking seekers is that the airframe is comparatively tiny. The two seekers need to be packaged within a narrow diameter [10] and in a way that provides gaps for both radio-frequency and IR energy (**Figure 4**).

The angular velocity of LoS is given in the next equation.

$$\omega_{LOS} = \frac{V}{\left|\vec{r}_{LOS}\right|} sin\left(\theta_{LOS} + \gamma\right); \theta_{LOS} = \arctan\left(\frac{Z}{D_R}\right)$$

There are many issues when the path to the target is defined only by elevation and azimuth from a UAV. The lightweight UAV moves at a relatively high velocity. During the flight, we can calculate several trajectories to the target, which should be

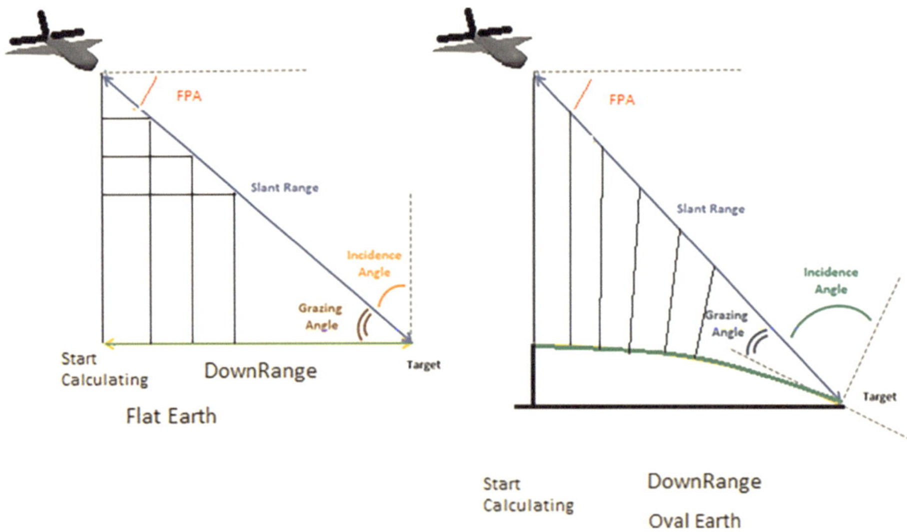

Figure 3.
General scheme of 6D trajectory.

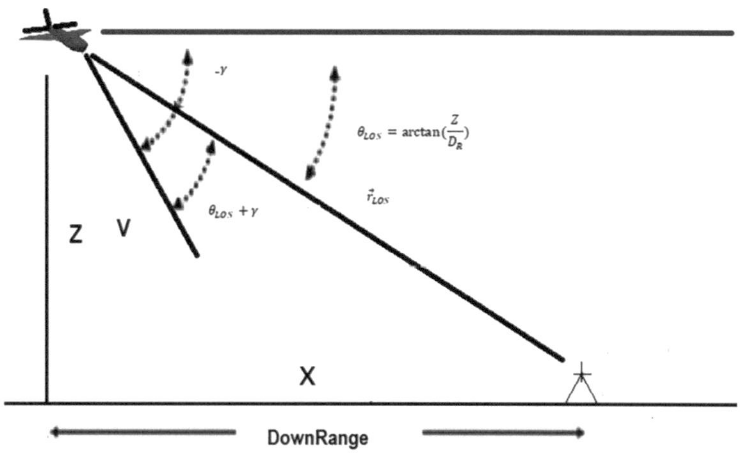

Figure 4.
2-D geometry of LoS—azimuth and elevation.

appraised using some criteria. Therefore, a decent algorithm is needed to compare the pre-calculated initial trajectories and remove the non-consistent ones. For example, the system could triangulate the target's position on the base of at least two trajectories, their initial positions, and the distance between initial positions.

For accuracy issues, it is beneficial for the flight path angle to follow the predefined trajectory very strictly and smoothly. The same approach could be applied to slow-moving targets, but then it should emit the signal permanently.

Unreliable measures of range, elevation, and azimuth to the target generated by ARTSD can occur in many cases; hence, it has fallen out of the scope of this research. ARTSD is supposed to continuously provide the flight control system with reliable information when the target radiates a signal.

The outputs from the passive radiation seeker are:

- Crossover Azimuth
- Crossover Elevation
- Range to the target—perchance

One of the key and obligatory elements is the altitude, measured by a barometric altimeter and GPS receiver.

6D trajectory consists of 3D position and attitude (roll, pitch, and yaw). To get some advantages of those six pre-calculated parameters, three significant problems arise:

- The moment the right 6D trajectory is calculated and how many times it should be calculated, the target stops and continues emitting several times. How to manage the set of pre-calculated 6D paths in case of multiple pre-calculated 6D trajectories
- Autopilot must take advantage of the 6D trajectory.
- Avoid or minimize all parallel movements along the 6D trajectory with standard aerodynamic control surfaces.

2. Aerodynamics of demonstrator

According to previous experience, initially predefined requirements the tandem fixed wing configuration was selected—**Figure 1**. The tandem aerodynamic configuration has acceptable oscillations in roll, pitch, and azimuth and good controllability. The tandem should be guided with big attention during the deep dives because both wings have almost the same lifting force.

2.1 Defining vehicle geometry

The relationship between the problematic feature (set of aerodynamics parameters) of medium-altitude-low-endurance, flight, and related platform response is determined with one purpose to have fewer oscillations generated by frame and smooth response with fewer overshoots.

An appropriate 3-D geometry model was developed in the environment of Fluent (ANSYS). The geometry of this tandem fixed-wing platform is described below. Potential performance requirements for this aircraft include an acceptable rate of climb and descent, level cruise speed, acceptable stall speed, and controllable low-level air velocity flight. The partial list of parameters for calculating the forces, moments, aerodynamic coefficients, and derivatives is given in **Table 1**.

The vehicle should have a stable and smooth flight. Basic responses to the commands should be out of oscillations

2.2 Determining vehicle aerodynamics and flight dynamics equation

Analytical prediction and simulations are a quicker and less expensive way to estimate aerodynamic characteristics in the early stages of design [2]. The airframe model incorporates several key assumptions and limitations: the airframe is a rigid body with constant mass, center of gravity, and inertia; ARTSD is a laterally symmetric vehicle; and control effectiveness varies nonlinearly with angle of attack and linearly with angle of deflection and air velocity. Control effectiveness is not dependent on sideslip angle because it is always very small.

Two flight dynamics models have been developed [2, 3]. The high-fidelity model is used to simulate and estimate the vehicle's behavior. The lower fidelity model estimates some flight parameters that should be used in AHRS and FLCS. The first one

ARTSD	Specifications
Wingspan (one wing)	0.75 m
Fuselage Length	0.65 m
Fuselage Diameter	0.08 m
Max Speed	230 km/h
Cruise Speed	140 km/h
Min Speed	30 km/h
Max Takeoff Weight	5 kg
FPA during terminal stage	$-3° \div -50°$

Table 1.
ARTSD geometry specifications.

precisely describes the behavior of the proposed dynamics configuration. The complex model is used in sFLCS (single STM32H750 processor). It could be run several times per standard time step (20 ms) for a closed-loop system. The second one is a subset of the first one and is much faster, and it does not allow missing performance during the defined flight envelope. The second one also is implemented in sFLCS. The high-fidelity simulation model's core is a nonlinear aircraft dynamics model (the first one) based on 12 ordinary differential equations and a large number of output equations. The main difference between those two models is the use of look up tables in the first and straightforward gains in the second. The complex model has been broken down into several standard subsystem modules, all of which are.

u, v, w—Body fixed linear velocity components in forward, side, and vertical directions, m/s;

$\dot{u}, \dot{v}, \dot{w}$—Linear accelerations, m/s^2;

X_a, Y_a, Z_a—Body forces per unit mass, N/kg;

p, q, r—Body fixed roll, pitch, and yaw rates;

g—Acceleration due to gravity, m/s^2;

Linear accelerations equations

$$\begin{aligned}\dot{u} &= rv - qw - g\sin\theta + X_a \\ \dot{v} &= pw - ru + g\sin\varphi\cos\theta + Y_a \\ \dot{w} &= qu - pv + g\cos\varphi\cos\theta + Z_a\end{aligned} \tag{1}$$

Angular accelerations equations

$$\begin{aligned}\dot{p} &= C_3L + C_4N + C_2pq + C_1qr \\ \dot{q} &= C_7M + C_6\left(p^2 - r^2\right) + C_5pr \\ \dot{r} &= C_4L + C_9N + C_8pq - C_2rq\end{aligned} \tag{2}$$

where,

$$\begin{gathered}C_1 = \left(\left(I_{yy} - I_{zz}\right)I_{zz} - I_{xz}^2\right)/\left(I_{xx}I_{zz} - I_{xz}^2\right) \\ C_2 = \left(I_{xx} - I_{yy} + I_{zz}\right)I_{zz}/\left(I_{xx}I_{zz} - I_{xz}^2\right) \\ C_3 = I_{zz}/\left(I_{xx}I_{zz} - I_{xz}^2\right) \\ C_4 = I_{xz}/\left(I_{xx}I_{zz} - I_{xz}^2\right) \\ C_5 = \left(I_{zz} - I_{xx}\right)/I_{yy} \\ C_6 = I_{xz}/I_{yy} \\ C_7 = 1/I_{yy} \\ C_8 = \left(I_{xx} - I_{yy}\right)1_{xx} + I_{xz}^2/\left(I_{xx}I_{zz} - I_{xz}^2\right) \\ C_9 = I_{xx}/\left(I_{xx}I_{zz} - I_{xz}^2\right)\end{gathered}$$

$\dot{p}, \dot{q}, \dot{r}$—roll, pitch, and yaw angular acceleration

I_{xx}, I_{yy}, I_{zz}—Moments of inertia about x, y, and z-axis, kg.m^2

L, M, N—Roll, pitch, and yaw moments about body axis, N. m;
The first derivatives of roll, pitch, and yaw are listed below:

$$\begin{aligned} \dot{\theta} &= q\cos\varphi - r\sin\varphi \\ \dot{\varphi} &= p + q\sin\varphi\tan\theta + r\cos\varphi\tan\theta \\ \dot{\psi} &= q\sin\varphi\sec\theta + r\cos\varphi\sec\psi\theta \end{aligned} \quad (3)$$

$$[X_a Y_a Z_a] = \frac{\bar{q}\,S}{\bar{m}}[C_X \;\; C_Y \;\; C_Z] \quad (4)$$

$$[L\,M\,N] = \bar{q}\,S\,[\,{}_bC_l \quad {}_cC_m \quad {}_bC_n\,] \quad (5)$$

$$C_x = -CX + CX_P - CX_Q\left(C_{X_q}\frac{q\bar{c}}{V}\right) + CX_R + CX_{ailP} + CX_{ailS} + CX_{elS} - CX_{elP} + CX_{rud} \quad (6)$$

$$C_y = CY + CY_P\left(C_{Y_p}\frac{p\bar{c}}{V}\right) + CY_Q - CY_R\left(C_{Y_r}\frac{r\bar{c}}{V}\right) + CY_{ailP} + CY_{ailS} + CY_{elP} - CY_{elS} + CY_{rud}$$

$$C_z = -CZ + CZ_P - CZ_Q\left(C_{Z_q}\frac{q\bar{c}}{V}\right) + CZ_R + CZ_{ailP} + CZ_{ailS} + CZ_{elP} - CZ_{elS} + CZ_{rud}$$

$$C_l = -Cl + Cl_P\left(C_{l_p}\frac{q\bar{c}}{V}\right) + Cl_Q + Cl_R\left(C_{l_r}\frac{q\bar{c}}{V}\right) - Cl_{ailP} - Cl_{ailS} + Cl_{elP} - Cl_{elS} + Cl_{rud}$$

$$C_m = -Cm - Cm_P + Cm_Q\left(C_{m_q}\frac{q\bar{c}}{V}\right) - Cm_R + Cm_{ailP} + Cm_{ailS} + Cm_{elP} - Cm_{elS} + Cm_{rud}$$

$$C_n = -Cn - Cn_P\left(C_{n_p}\frac{q\bar{c}}{V}\right) + Cn_Q + Cn_R\left(C_{n_r}\frac{q\bar{c}}{V}\right) - Cn_{ailP} - Cn_{ailS} + Cn_{elP} - Cn_{elS} + Cn_{rud}$$

The block diagram of the complex flight dynamics model is shown in **Figure 5**. AoA setup block creates an artificial angle of attack here, and it has been used in pFLCS and MBC tuning procedures. Front and aft wings of tandem have ailerons,

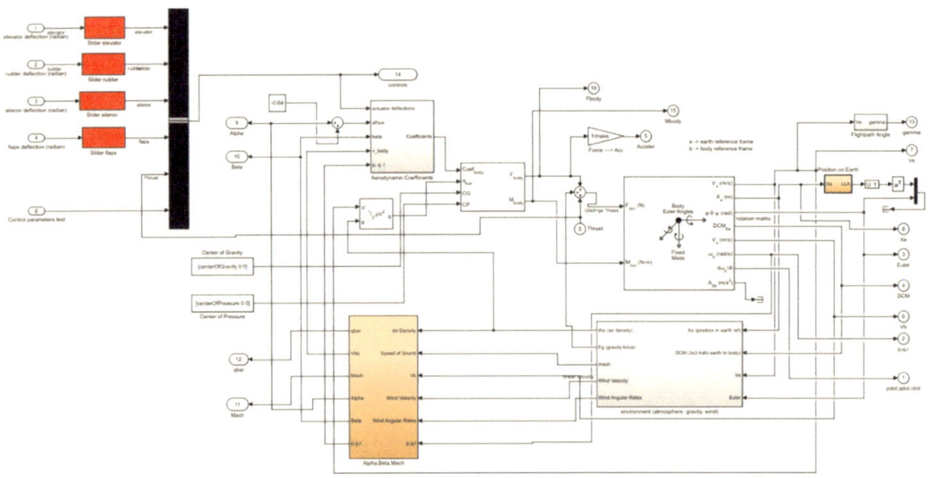

Figure 5.
General flight dynamics block diagram.

elevators, rudder, and flaps. The second version of the "Aerodynamic Coefficients" block was developed when the control surfaces were elevons and rudders [11]. pFLCS (another STM32H750 processor) calculates separate aileron and elevator commands and mixes them in one joint elevator command. When the mixed command is used, a deep dive is better done with elevons and flaps.

2.3 Aerodynamics coefficients for constructing forces and moments

Tandem aircraft can be considered as ordinary fixed-wing UAVs [3, 5, 6]. The flight dynamics model consists of several subsystems, such as equations of motion, environmental models, calculation of aerodynamic coefficients, forces, and moments, environmental models, alpha, beta, and Mach aerodynamic coefficients, and forces and moments. All look-up tables calculated by Fluent (ANSYS) are implemented in the flight model. A body fixed reference frame specifies forces, moments, and angles [12]. Primary control surfaces are elevators, ailerons, flaps, and the rudder. Ultimately, flaps, elevons, and rudder were used instead and tested successfully.

3. Design of 3D trajectory

Design and usage of 6D trajectory is important part of control topologies investigated here. As it was mentioned, here more complex way is used to calculate 6D trajectory, which increases the accuracy at the final stage. This is the simplest formulation, which ignores wind, spin, and drag.

Standard ray-tracing procedure is used for calculation initial 6D trajectory Equations (7 and 8). That will calculates the positions, elevations, and azimuth of a ray of points connecting the current position of the vehicle with the possible position of the target somewhere along the ray. The advantage of this procedure, avoids any parallel longitudinal or lateral motions along the ray.

$$\begin{aligned} \Delta X_n &= step.cos\,(El_n).\sin(Az_n) \\ \Delta Y_n &= step.cos\,(El_n).\cos(Az_n) \\ \Delta \mathrm{Z_n} &= \mathrm{step.\,sin(El_n)} \end{aligned} \tag{7}$$

$$\begin{aligned} \mathrm{X_n} &= \mathrm{X_{n-1}} + \Delta \mathrm{X_{n-1}} \\ Y_n &= Y_{n-1} + \Delta Y_{n-1} \\ \mathrm{Z_n} &= \mathrm{Z_{n-1}} + \Delta \mathrm{Z_{n-1}} \end{aligned} \tag{8}$$

The generation of 6D trajectory has two real-time vital procedures:

- Calculate the initial and linear ray pointing to the target according to radiation seeker outputs, GPS, and barometric altimeter

- Recalculate the linear trajectory, depending on the requirements for final approach maneuvers.

The straight-line 6D trajectory is pre-calculated and stored in the "3D Position Trajectory" block. It should be modified to fit the requirements of the final approach to the target—steep dive, for example. The requirements could be a steep dive, almost vertical dive, or low-altitude approach. The example given below considers a dive to the target at the final stage.

Finally, the required gamma and azimuth will be calculated along the initially computed linear 6D trajectory. Even if the platform has some parallel motion in lateral or longitudinal planes; the proposed approach will give demands to pFLCS to remove that parallel motion. The new correct demands of Gamma and Azimuth will be calculated to follow the initial 6D path—see **Figure 6**.

Some simple procedures could be used to calculate the final trajectory maneuvers in the block "Special Shape Generator":

- First-order systems;
- Predefined trapezoid;
- High-order discrete filter.

A very simple rule has been used to have a consistent final trajectory, depicted in **Figure 7**. Two points along the initial linear trajectory are selected: *Start Point* and *End Point*. The positions and attitudes of those two points are not changeable, but any points in the interval, defined by them along the ray, could be changed according to the requirements of special maneuvering. Before the End Point or after it, we should have a few points very close to it. That will minimize the transition process and make it smoother.

Figures 7–9 show the process of trajectory design.

The same approach could be used for lateral 6D trajectory, if a special maneuver is required.

Part of offensive and evasive maneuvers, used to create the decent 6D trajectory are listed below:

- Deep dive at final approach
- Very low leveled flight to the target
- Normal approach (FPA =30°).

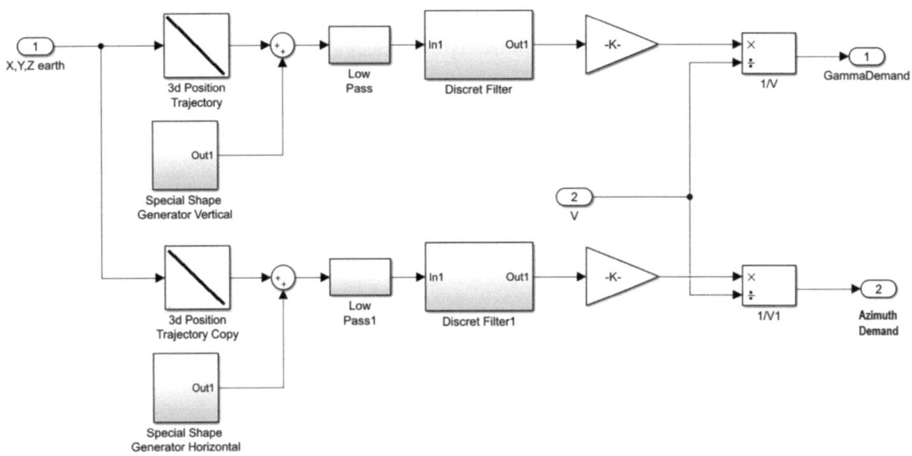

Figure 6.
Block diagram of calculation of 6D trajectory—6D slope subsystem.

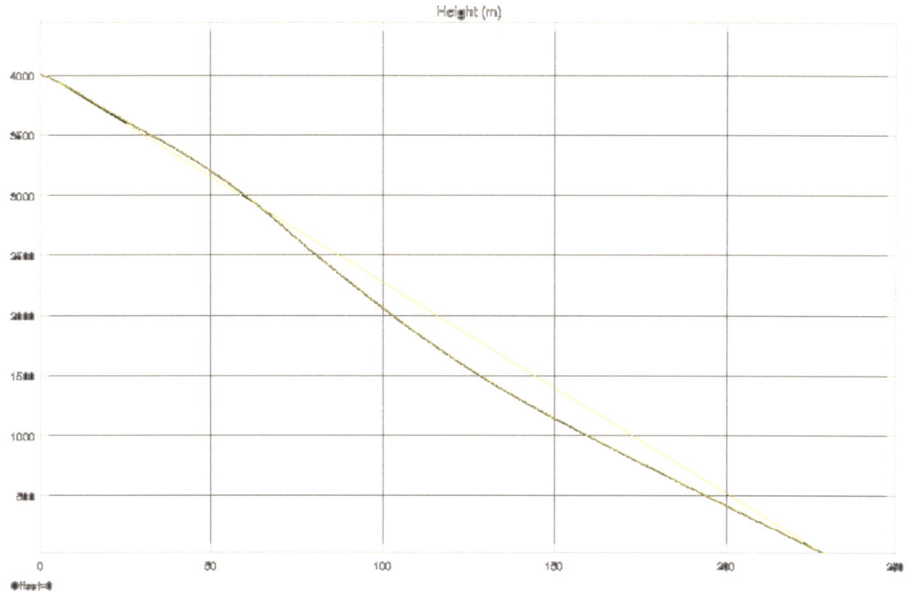

Figure 7.
The initial straight line of pre-calculated trajectory and final trajectory.

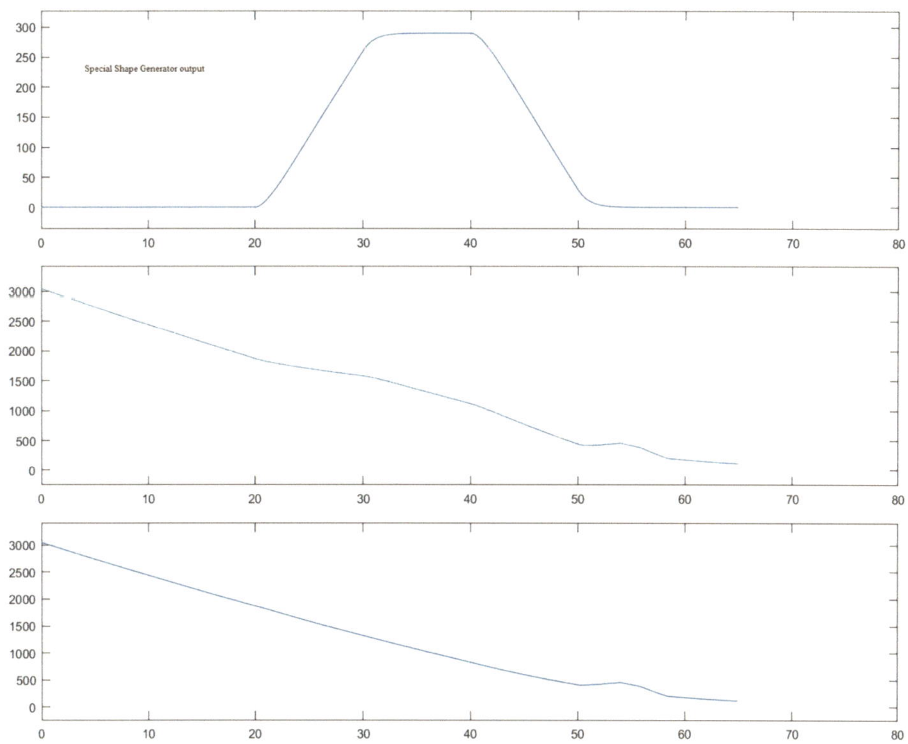

Figure 8.
Output from the special shape generator and how it is added to the final trajectory.

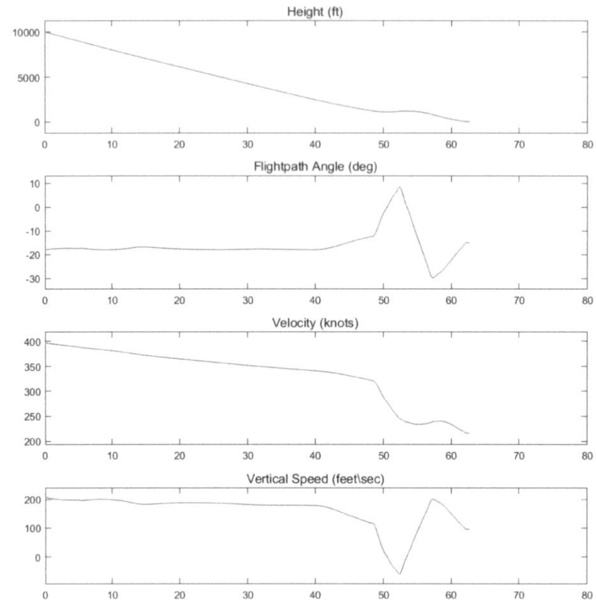

Figure 9.
Non-compensated dynamic response to final trajectory.

4. Model based control

The casual approach is used for 3-loops autopilot [6], where platform longitudinal dynamics can be defined by the short-period approximation of the longitudinal equations of motion. Inscribed in state space from the basic longitudinal platform is

$$\dot{\mathrm{x}} = \mathrm{Ax} + \mathrm{Bu}$$
$$\mathrm{y} = \mathrm{Cx} + \mathrm{Du}$$

where

$$x = \begin{bmatrix} \alpha \\ q \end{bmatrix}, u = \delta_p, y = \begin{bmatrix} A_{zp} \\ q_p \end{bmatrix}$$

The more specifics the short-period dynamics are

$$A = \begin{bmatrix} \frac{1}{V_{p0}} \left[\frac{\overline{Q}SC_{z\alpha0}}{m} - A_{x0} \right] & 1 \\ \frac{\overline{Q}SdC_{m\alpha0}}{I_{yy}} & 0 \end{bmatrix}, B = \begin{bmatrix} \frac{\overline{Q}SC_{z\delta p0}}{mV_{p0}} \\ \frac{\overline{Q}SdC_{m\delta p0}}{I_{yy}} \end{bmatrix}$$

$$C = \begin{bmatrix} \frac{\overline{Q}SC_{z\alpha0}}{mg} - \frac{\overline{Q}SdC_{m\alpha p0}}{gI_{yy}}\overline{x} & 0 \\ 0 & 1 \end{bmatrix}, D = \begin{bmatrix} \frac{\overline{Q}SC_{z\delta p0}}{mg} - \frac{\overline{Q}SdC_{m\delta p0}}{gI_{yy}}\overline{x} \\ 0 \end{bmatrix}$$

Upon combining "trajectory geometry feedback" equations with the laws of guidance, the munitions' trajectory is found to be given in terms of two independent linear differential equations of identical form and of one higher order than the vehicle transfer function [6]. That involves some complications because we are forced to work with a linearized model with minor deviations, leading to unexpected behavior. Successful real-time implementation of trajectory guidance algorithms has employed precise methods that either assume some knowledge of flight mechanics or make assumptions to reduce the dimensionality of the dynamical system [13].

The novel approach proposed in Refs. [2, 3] is modified and refined to create appropriate behavior for the platform. It is intuitive and robust. The proposed MBC approach is easily deployed in both lateral and longitudinal channels, as we see in several different topologies. The concept of the proposed MBC [2–4] is slightly different because of the other tasks to be performed and includes two specific basic steps, which are different in detail for each application: design the reference trajectory or required response and create the model following the controller. The model-based control concept fits with the current trajectory following the procedure. The advantages of the proposed algorithm are:

- No need for initial simplification of flight dynamics
- The procedure for tuning control parameters is offline and intuitive-complete search for optimal solution.
- Robust control of the changes in flight parameters and environment
- Fast response with minimal oscillations
- The response of a closed-loop system could be shaped in many different ways.

Figure 10 depicts the common block diagram of a 2-loop MBC autopilot with angular position and velocity. Two reference models of angle and its angular rate are used to determine the closed-loop system response. We have two feedback signals of the measured angle and its rate. The outputs of the reference model are delivered as feedback to two serial basic angle and angle rate loops.

The last step is to design a control law, which follows with minimal or zero error the modified 6D trajectory. Five different topologies have been used and they are described below.

Topology 1: The approach is a combination of 3-loops autopilot and 2-loops MBC control. The turn is made by ailerons

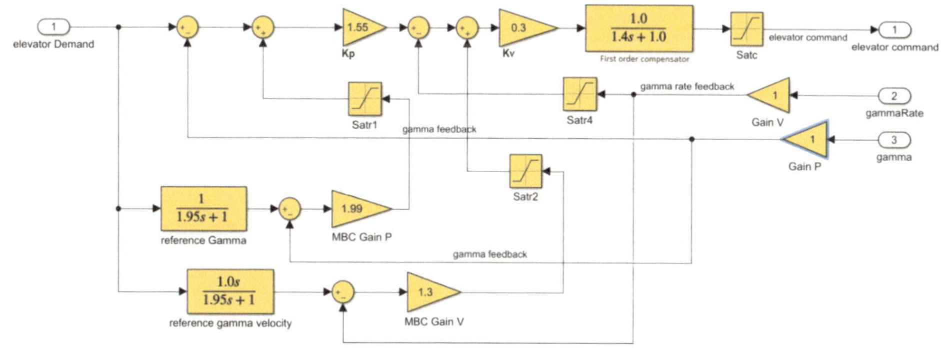

Figure 10.
Block diagram for longitudinal model-based control.

Longitudinal channel

$$e_{1e} = K_{\gamma}(\gamma_{des} - \gamma)$$
$$e_{2e} = K_{Az}(e_{1e} - A_z)$$
$$e_{3e} = K_q(e_{2e} - q)$$

$\delta_e = K_e(e_{3e} - \theta)$, here the 2-loop MBC is implemented
lateral channel

$$e_{1a} = K_{\beta}(\beta_{des} - \beta)$$
$$e_{2a} = K_{Ay}(e_{1a} - A_y)$$
$$e_{3e} = K_p(e_{2a} - p)$$

$\delta_a = K_a(e_{3a} - \varphi)$, here the 2-loop MBC is implemented

$$G(s) = \frac{1}{T_a s + k_a}, \text{ compensator transfer function for both channels}$$

Topology 2: The same as Topology 1, but the input is roll angle.
The longitudinal channel is the same.
Lateral channel control law

$$e_{1a} = K_{\beta}(\beta_{des} - \varphi)$$
$$e_{2a} = K_{Ay}(e_{1a} - A_y)$$
$$e_{3e} = K_p(e_{2a} - p)$$

$\delta_a = K_a(e_{3a} - \varphi)$, here the 2-loop MBC is applied

$$G(s) = \frac{1}{T_a s + k_a}, \text{ compensator transfer function}$$

In order to ensure the qualitative transient process of the closed-loop system we need the following conditions

$$\lim_{s \to 0} \frac{A_{zp}}{A_{zc}} = 1, \text{ or } \lim_{s \to 0} \dot{\gamma} = 0, \text{ or } \lim_{s \to 0} \frac{\gamma_{zp}}{\gamma_{zc}} = 1$$

Here, the input to the reference model is "elevator demand," but it could be pitch demand. The reference model has two feedback signals: proportional (pitch) and velocity (pitch rate), as shown in **Figure 10**. The exact configuration could be used for flight path angle and flight path angle rate. Of course, you need more processor time to calculate the flight path angle, which is acceptable for the current FLCS processor configuration. Therefore, the proposed MBC also has two modest gains: proportional and velocity (longitudinal channel).

$$K_p = (P_{min}, P_{max})$$

Step 1: Determine the boundary conditions and the steps of all tuned parameters – two sets of (k_{rp}, k_{rv})
Step 2: Decide if the trimming procedure is needed and where it will be placed
Step 3: Determine the initial states for all tuned parameters
Step 4: Determine initial flight conditions and need angle of attack to be included in tuning as a parameter
Step 5: Run full-scale search nested loops
Step 6: Calculate the transition process for each set of tuned parameters. Remember the best three solutions according to the chosen criteria.
Step 7: Stop when a complete full-scale search is handled

Table 2.
Steps of tuning procedure for MBC.

$$K_v = (V_{min}, V_{max})$$

The ranges of feedback gains, describing the influence of position and velocity reference models, are defined in the following way:

$$K_{rp} = (RP_{min}, RP_{max}); K_{rv} = (RV_{min}, RV_{max}); K_{ar} = (AR_{min}, AR_{max}) \text{ if needed}$$

The steps of gain changes are determined as d_p, d_v, d_{rp}, and d_{rv}. In addition, for each range, a step dpp and dvp is defined. The current correction procedure consists of in our case four nested loops, which move the current values of the gains: K_p, K_v, K_{rp}, and K_{rv} with appropriate steps d_p, d_v, d_{rp}, and d_{rv}.

This governs the simple algorithm doing a full-scale search through the ranges of the gains and parameters. During the run-time, the parameters of each transition-time process or frequency domain and time domain characteristics, are evaluated, and the best solution according to the proper criteria is chosen and stored. Each loop corresponds to the specific gain or parameter (which could be the limits for saturations, for example) of the MBC. The number of loops is equivalent to the number of gains and parameters determined by the structure of MBC.

Several limitation parameters in the position, velocity, and acceleration loops could be defined appropriately and added to the procedure search if needed. The same approach could be used for trimming the platform, and it could be done before the tuning of FLCS or by adding some nested loops in the procedure of FLCS shaping. That is a numerical solution for complex nonlinear dynamics, and it avoids stopping at the local extremum. The time required for calculations depends on the complexity of flight dynamics models. The procedure for tuning the MBC behavior consists of the following steps in **Table 2**.

The primary step in the procedure is Step 5, but Step 6 consumes most of the calculation time. Occasionally, the more significant order of nested loops (or input parameters) could affect the final result. It does not frequently happen, but should be mentioned (**Figure 11**).

4.1 Adaptive and gain-schedule model-based control

MBC design and tuning are subject to the present configuration and the number of parameters included in the nested loops, because of that two cases in the gain-scheduled MBC were examined:

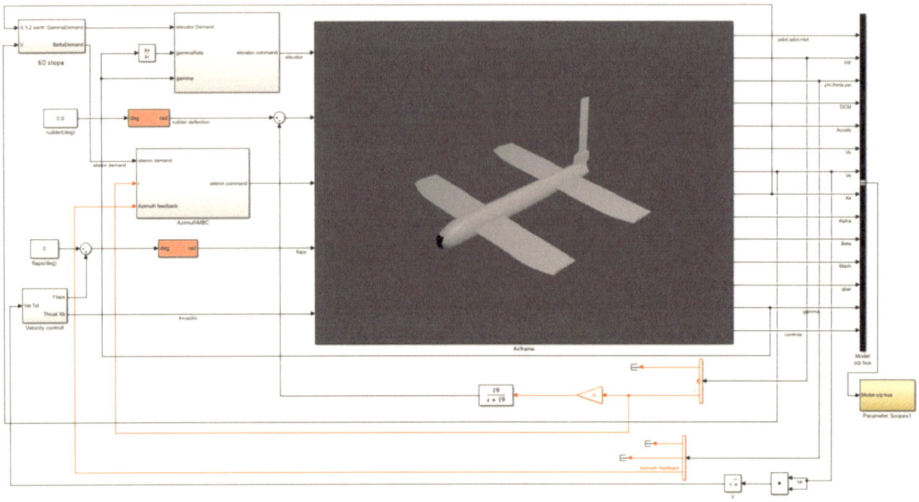

Figure 11.
Overall simulation solution, Topology 1 and 2.

- Gain-scheduling for feedback gains of the reference model and parameters of MBC
- Gain-scheduling for gains or parameters of proportional and velocity serial loops of MBC.

The range of used reference models is broad enough. The non-minimal phase behavior of the platform could be controlled with appropriate MBC, which is proven in Ref. [2]; then we will have a normal minimal phase behavior. Even an appropriate reference model could transform a minimal-phase system into a non-minimal-phase one. Deep dive and high angle of attack flights of tailless and tandem airframes cause non-minimal phase behavior at the beginning of transient response—opposite to the input signal glitch. That negative glitch could significantly affect the required transition process. The typical transfer function for non-minimal phase behavior is shown in the next equation

$$F_{gNMP}(s) = \frac{(s - z_1(t))(s + z_2(t))}{(s^2 + A(t)s + B(t))}$$

It is appropriate to use gain scheduling for some of the gains of FLCS along with air velocity, altitude, and AoA. Generally, time-variant parameters of the reference model should be included in the nested loops of the procedure as inputs with their ranges or look-up tables. In this case, the gain will be a look-up table with the inputs of AoA and total air velocity and altitude. The best selection criteria and parameters of the transition process are multifaceted. Here, we have another option to solve the desired AoA problem. We can use the AoA setup block (see **Figure 3**), which was added to the simulation solution. That block aims to change the AoA along the tuning procedure easily. An additional nested loop should be added for artificially generated AoA and its change step to the procedure. This approach approves almost the entire AoA range of change is covered and investigated.

The simplified version of gain-scheduled model-based control includes only two look-up tables. Respectively, they replace K_p and K_v forward gains. The time for tuning the parameters here is much shorter. The reference model could be a variation of the flight dynamics model with different levels of detail in more multifaceted cases.

Here, the principal steps in the tuning algorithm are the same as stated in **Table 2**. The new parameters mentioned above should be added as inputs, limit steps, and nested loops. The main advantage of this self-tuning procedure is that it will calculate the global extremum and will not stop at some local extremum. Also, it will calculate the MBC according to the high-fidelity nonlinear dynamics. The process is lengthy, and for more intricate flight dynamics, it can take over 56 hours to determine the best set of control law parameters. The benefits become clear when dealing with nonlinear flight dynamics, where look-up tables are preferred over formulas. The same procedure could be applied to sliding mode control and inverse dynamic control with nonlinear dynamics [1, 14, 15].

According to the chosen aerodynamic configuration, the sideslip angle β is assumed to be zero, which reduces the calculation time. When the almost skid-to-turn algorithm is used, it will be included as input into the nested loops, spreading the time for finding a complete solution.

The MBC provides similar behaviors as those found with the more complex algorithms lake LQG control but has the benefits of a simplified and more intuitive scheme, even when the saturation parameters are added to dynamic parameters of position, velocity, and acceleration reference systems [2]. The process of tuning an MBC reduces to adjusting a simple reference 'bandwidth' to achieve the desired performance for the specific vehicle. The design of the controller has two key elements:

- Tuning the parameters of the controller
- Outcomes performance-relevant reference system dynamics.

The initial version of really flying ARTSD was produced alongside the simulation environment, conferring the geometry parameters in **Table 2**. Once a control-relevant model is derived, tuning the MBC is relatively straightforward. Some preliminary flights were done with a flying demonstrator without a radiation seeker, where the azimuth and elevation demands generated by the" 6D Slope" subsystem or their derivatives were the input to model-based control.

The platform descends from 4000 m to sea level height, and because of that, the system needs auto trimming or gain scheduling [2–4]. The same procedure of tuning MBC is used to solve the problem, but the height range is split into four subranges (4000–3000), (3000–2000), (2000–1000), and (1000–0). There is a separate evaluation of the transition process and different best solution variables for all those ranges. Generally, we will have a look-up table (5x1) instead of a simple coefficient for each shaped gain in MBC. The transition between gains, defined in look-up tables as a function of altitude, AoA, and air velocity, is smooth or fast—less than 0.3 se.

The tuning procedure for MBC will last about 18 hours. We should consider reasonable accuracy assumptions in the number of gains, gain steps, and the total time of the transition process (an average of 80 sec.). The gain-scheduled procedure with altitude ranges, AoA, or air velocity dependency will at least double the time.

4.2 "Inverse Inverse" flight dynamics control

The idea of deploying "inverse inverse" dynamics control [2, 3] is to use a simplified or qualitative forward flight dynamics model, described later in the same chapter, in a recursive procedure of full-scale search to calculate control surface demands according to forces, moments and flight parameters. The term "inverse inverse" dynamics concisely conveys the essence of the algorithm. We do not need cumbersome complex analytical calculations or simplifications leading to a loss of accuracy. Double inverse means forward but used in a different way with full-scale search and nested loops. Let us say the acceleration demand *xademand* along the vertical axe Z in the body frame is somehow determined. Control surface deflection should be determined according to simplified or precise flight dynamics. The ranges of control surface deflections are defined in the following way

$$\delta_e = (\delta_{e\,\min}, \delta_{e\,\max}); \delta_a = (\delta_{a\,\min}, \delta_{a\,\max}); \qquad (9)$$
$$\delta_r = (\delta_{r\,\min}, \delta_{r\,\max}); \delta_f = (\delta_{f\,\min}, \delta_{f\,\max});$$

For each range is defined a step Δ. The selected input parameters determine four nested loops in the general case of Eq. (9). The full-scale search through the ranges of input control deflections consists of four nested loops for each control, which move the current values of the deflections with the appropriate steps. After completing the procedure, the appropriate values for control surfaces $(\delta_a{}^l, \delta_e{}^i, \delta_f{}^j, \delta_r{}^k)$, will be found to satisfy in the best way Eq. (10). Each time step, we should calculate Eq. (11), along the nested loop.

$$X_a{}^{demand} = \frac{\bar{q}\,S}{\bar{m}} C_{X_n}(\alpha^m, \beta^m, \delta_a{}^l, \delta_e{}^i, \delta_f{}^j, \delta_r{}^k, V, h) \qquad (10)$$

Generally, elevator command will be calculated with the full-scale search and forward dynamics according to Eq. (11) but will be equivalent to the result of inverse dynamics.

$$\delta_e = f(X_a{}^{demand}, M^{demand}) \qquad (11)$$

Simply we calculate acceleration equations for each value of control surfaces, gradually according to nested loops, that are to find the closest acceleration X_a to acceleration demand $X_a{}^{demand}$.

$$[X_a Y_a Z_a] = \frac{\bar{q}\,S}{\bar{m}}[C_{X_n}, C_{Y_n}, C_{Z_n}]$$
$$[L\,M\,N] = \bar{q}\,S\,[bC_{l_n}, cC_{m_n}, bC_{n_n}] \qquad (12)$$

Subscript n means iteration in searching procedure. Parameters α^m, β^m are optional and they could be values measured by sensors of the platform. Equations (13 and 14) are final versions of linear and angular equations. If we need angular accelerations, we must calculate Eq. (14).

$$C_{X_n} = C_{X_n}(\alpha^m, \beta^m, \delta_a{}^l, \delta_e{}^i, \delta_r{}^k, V, h);$$
$$C_{Y_n} = C_{Y_n}(\alpha^m, \beta^m, \delta_a{}^l, \delta_e{}^i, \delta_r{}^k, V, h);$$
$$C_{Z_n} = C_{Z_a}(\alpha^m, \beta^m, \delta_a{}^l, \delta_e{}^i, \delta_r{}^k, V, h); \qquad (13)$$
$$C_{l_n} = C_{l_n}(\alpha^m, \beta^m, \delta_a{}^l, \delta_e{}^i, \delta_r{}^k, V, h);$$
$$C_{m_n} = C_{m_n}(\alpha^m, \beta^m, \delta_a{}^l, \delta_e{}^i, \delta_r{}^k, V, h);$$
$$C_{n_n} = C_{n_n}(\alpha^m, \beta^m, \delta_a{}^l, \delta_e{}^i, \delta_r{}^k, V, h); \qquad (14)$$

There are two ways to calculate inverse inverse dynamics:

- Calculate the entire set of 12 ODE
- Calculate the linear and angular accelerations (4–6).

In the article, the second approach is used.

The real-time algorithm of the inverse flight dynamics calculation consists of three steps.

Step 1: Find solution through full-scale search along the control demands

$$\dot{x}(t) = f(x(t), \delta(t)) \rightarrow X_a{}^{demand} = \frac{\bar{q}\,S}{\bar{m}} C_{X_n}\left(\alpha^m, \beta^m, \delta_a{}^l, \delta_e{}^i, \delta_r{}^k, V, h\right)$$

$$\left[\delta_a{}^l, \delta_e{}^i, \delta_r{}^k, V, h\right] = > C_{X_n}^{numerical}\left(\alpha^m, \beta^m, \delta_a{}^l, \delta_e{}^i, \delta_r{}^k, V, h, \tilde{X}_a{}^{demand}\right)$$

Step 2: Calculate the Equation of Motion; the next equation is one of the possible solutions.

$$\left[\delta_a{}^l, \delta_e{}^i, \delta_r{}^k, p, q, r, \gamma, \varphi, \theta, \psi, V, h\right] = > F\left(\alpha^m, \beta^m, \delta_a{}^l, \delta_e{}^i, \delta_r{}^k, V, h, \tilde{X}_a{}^{demand}\right)$$

Step 3: Calculate the inverse dynamics controller.

During *Step 1* it will not be always, possible to find the exact solution $\left[\delta_a{}^l, \delta_e{}^i, \delta_r{}^k, V, h\right]$ so the decision will be the nearest to $X_a{}^{demand}$ or $\tilde{X}_a{}^{demand}$ according to the smallest error.

Calculation of Equations of Motion requires a lot of microprocessor power, so it should be used with caution. In the current research, it is used once to calculate directly desired pitch angle. Proper evaluation of pitch angle requires calculations of several time steps.

The inverse dynamics approach could be used with a complete nonlinear flight model; of course, if enough processor power is available. The full nonlinear model with look-up tables has been tested on an STM32H750 microprocessor and run time was 1.2 ms. Sometimes the accelerations are not properly estimated. We can really have

$$X_a{}^{demand} \approx X_a \tag{15}$$

because of the step moving forward the control surfaces. The usages of faster microprocessors allow frequent use of complete FAD.

The process of Step 1 is the fastest and requires 0.01 ms, which is not bad and allows 2000 cycles along the nested loop when the normal control loop takes 20 ms. This amount of cycles allows to use of very small steps and that will neglect the problem of Eq. (15). The separate STM32H750 processor is used to calculate inverse inverse dynamics in both versions, light and complete.

The ranges of control surface deflections of FLCS are defined in Eq. (9).

Table 3 describes the main sequence of the tuning procedure.

Step 8. It needs additional explanation in the particular case of topology 4 use of "Inverse, Inverse Dynamics". The output of the block will require angular and linear accelerations pitch angle θ_{Azi} (longitudinal channel). Here, we have two cases. The first is to calculate several steps of the transition process, which will be enough because the pitch angle will be passed to MBC as a demand. The second case is to calculate the pitch angle for a longer periodθAzi; then, we will have a smoother and faster process.

Step 1: Determine the boundary conditions and steps of all tuned parameters—two sets of (δ_e, δ_a). Determine whether α is a constant or will be changed during the procedure
Step 2: Determine the initial conditions for all tuned parameters
Step 3: Determine flight conditions and need angle of attack to be included in tuning as a parameter
Step 4: Run the full-search nested loops, which changes step by step the tuned parameters of FAD
Step 5: Store the best values of linear and angular accelerations for each subrange
Step 6: Stop the nested loops
Step 7: Calculate several time steps of the transition process for each set of best-tuned parameters. Remember the best three solutions according to the chosen criteria.

Table 3.
Steps of tuning procedure for "Inverse, Inverse Dynamics and Control".

Inverse, inverse model-based control consists of three main blocks:

- Full-scale search—the module has several multiple lops for each of the tunable parameters—FSS
- Forward aero dynamics—FAD, the same diagram as **Figure 3** is used as the FAD subsystem
- Calculator of required demands—control surface deflections or demands. Required demands are calculated according to inputs of FAD and required linear

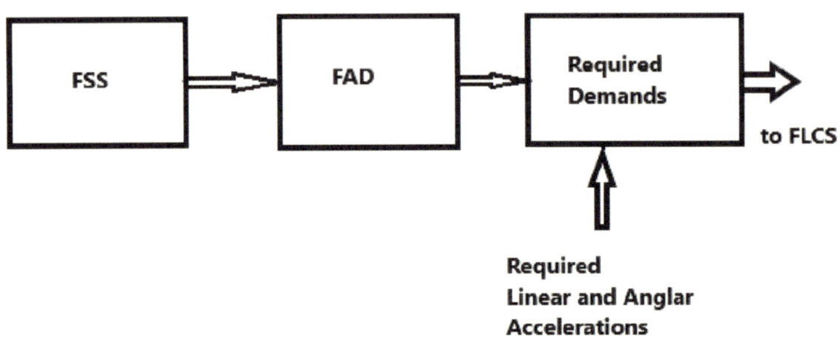

Figure 12.
That is for inverse inverse control.

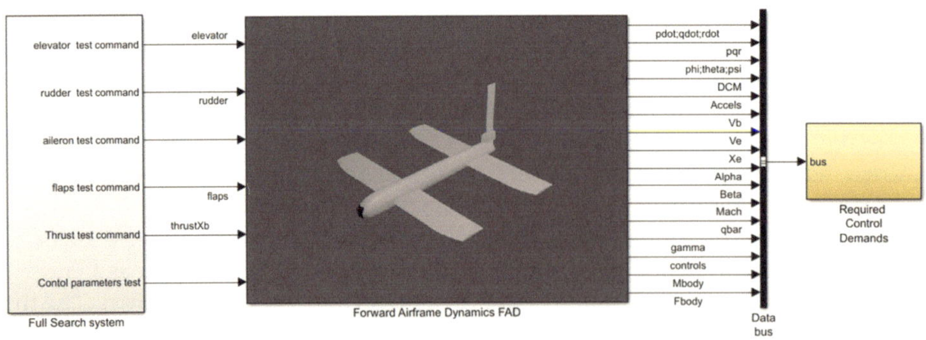

Figure 13.
Block diagram of IIDC.

Flight dynamics model (almost high-fidelity, 32 look-up tables) appropriate.	0.04 ms
Model-based control with reference model (position, velocity, and acceleration), and removing the Gravity (steep turns).	0.01 ms

Table 4.
Performance of AHRS/FLCS processor (STM32H750 processor).

and angular accelerations, pitch, pitch rate, roll, and FPA—required demands. The block calculates demands according to the current state of the platform and pre-calculated 6D trajectory.

The general diagram of the proposed IIDC is depicted in **Figure 12**.

FAD subsystem is identical dynamics depicted in **Figure 3**, if needed some additional inputs and outputs are complemented. The topology IIDC used here is shown in **Figure 13**.

The AHRS [16, 17] and FLCS were built on STM32H750, and some performance tests are listed in **Table 4**. Several output signals, coming from FAD could be used to augment the stability and accuracy of AHRS, linear and angular accelerations, roll, pitch, and yaw rates as well as roll, pitch, and yaw [18].

The main control topologies with IIDC are explained below.

Topology 3: MBC + inverse dynamics:

Longitudinal channel:

$$e_{1e} = K_\gamma(\gamma_{des} - \gamma)$$

$$e_{2e} = K_{Az}(e_{1e} - A_z) \text{ Inverse inverse dynamics calculate } A_z \text{ and } \theta_{Azi}$$

$$e_{3e} = K_q(e_{2e} - q)$$

$$\delta_e = K_{fa}(e_{3e} - \theta_{Azi}), \text{here the } 2 - \text{loop MBC is implemented}$$

Inverse inverse dynamics calculate A_z and θ_{Azi}. In that case, the entire forward flight dynamics model should use pitch.

$$K_q(e_{2e} - q)$$

$$e_{4e} = K_{fa}(e_{3e} - \theta_{Azi})$$

$$G(s) = \frac{1}{T_a s + k_a}, \text{compensator transfer function}$$

Lateral channel:

$$e_{1a} = K_\beta(\beta_{des} - \beta)$$

$$e_{2a} = K_{Ay}(e_{1a} - A_{yi}) \text{ Inverse inverse dynamics calculate } A_{yi} \text{ and } \varphi_{Ayi}$$

$$e_{3e} = K_p(e_{2a} - p)$$

$$\delta_a = K_a(e_{3a} - \varphi), \text{here the } 2 - \text{loop MBC is implemented}$$

$$G(s) = \frac{1}{T_a s + k_a}, \text{compensator transfer function for both channels}$$

The final topology examined here is the so-called skid-to-turn control with or without IIDC just for lateral channel [19, 20]. “Skid-to-turn” control could be used

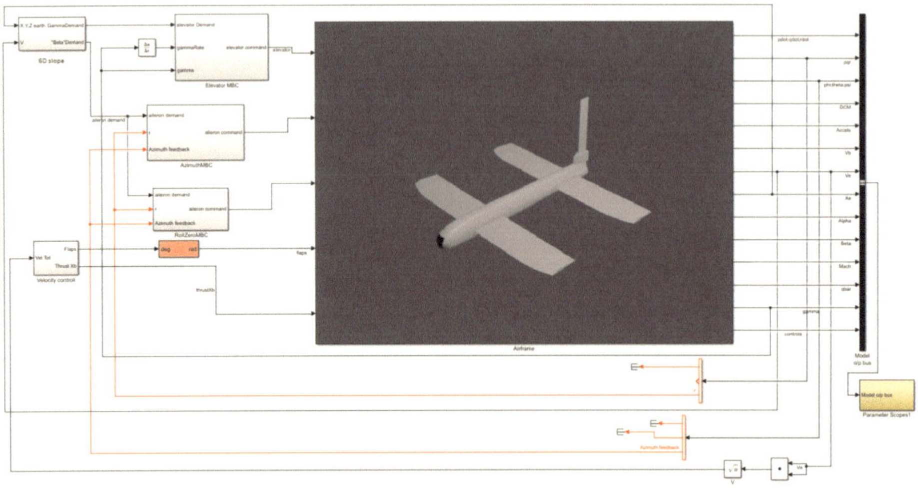

Figure 14.
General "Skid to Turn" with MBC (IIDC is not shown here).

successfully with all discussed topologies. The idea is to rudder for azimuth control and ailerons to keep the roll angle equal to zero.

Topology 4: Skid to turn with MBC for lateral channel
lateral channel control law.

$$e_{1r} = K_\beta\left(\beta_{des} - A_{yi}\right), A_{yi} \text{ is calculated by IID}$$

$$e_{1r} = K_p(e_{1r} - r)$$

$$\delta_r = K_a(e_{2r} - \text{azimuth})$$

$$G(s) = \frac{1}{T_a s + k_a}, \text{compensator transfer function}$$

The block diagram of **Figure 14** shows the common usage of "skid-to-turn" with MBC and eventually IIDC. The difference between those two topologies is the presence or absence of IIDC in the blocks "ElevatorMBC", "AzimuthMBC", and "RollZeroMBC".

An advanced approach for the determination of platform attitude is used to enhance the accuracy of guidance.

5. Simulation results

Analysis of simulation results in the current work is focused on the qualitative aspects of the obtained transient responses with respect to particular control topology(s). The MBC works well with a proposed approach of using FLCS.

The reference model should be selected cautiously because there are some physical limitations, which could not be implemented. The procedure of selecting a reference model might require several passes. The aerodynamics of the platform and the proposed reference models transient processes have been simulated in several situations:

- Topology 5—Skid-To-turn + MBC without turbulence—**Figure 15**

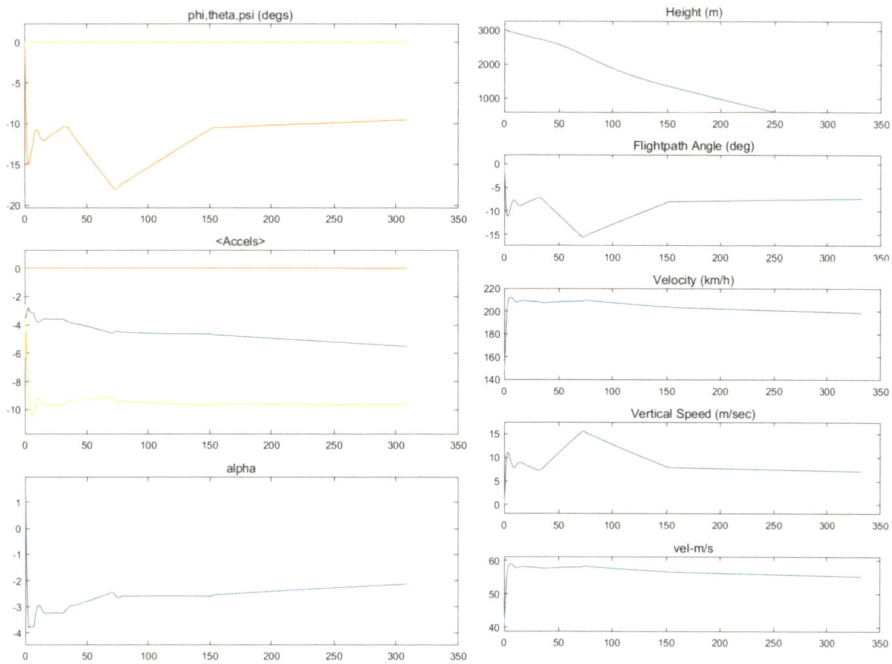

Figure 15.
Skid-To-turn + MBC without turbulence.

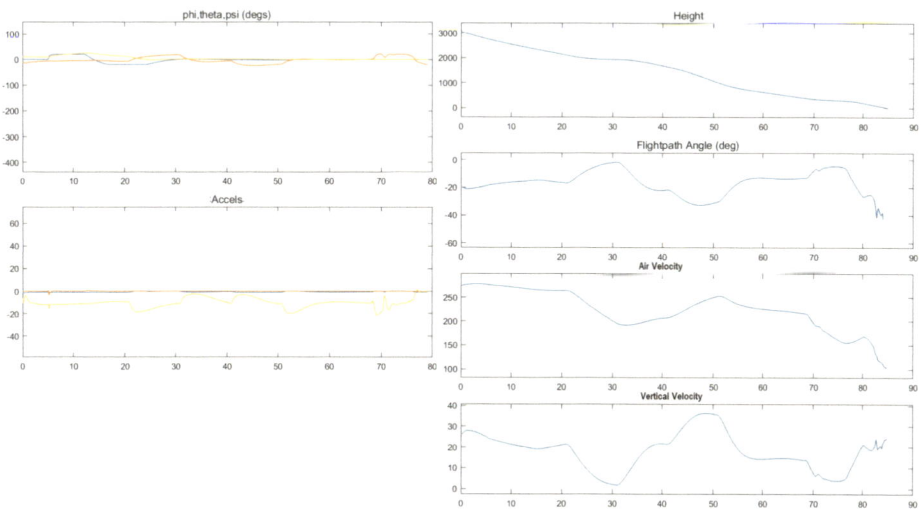

Figure 16.
Skid to Turn + MBC simulation results, with lateral maneuvers.

- Topology 5—Skid to Turn + MBC simulation results, with lateral maneuvers—**Figure 16**
- Topology 5—Skid-to-Turn and MBC with turbulence—**Figure 17**
- Topology 1 with turbulence—**Figure 18**

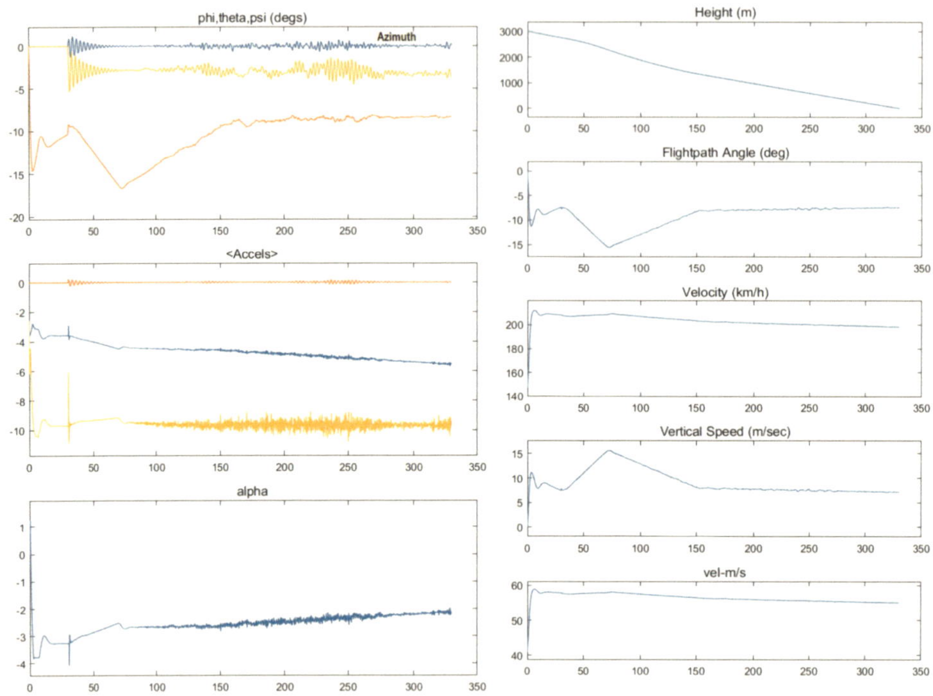

Figure 17.
Skid-to-Turn and MBC with turbulence.

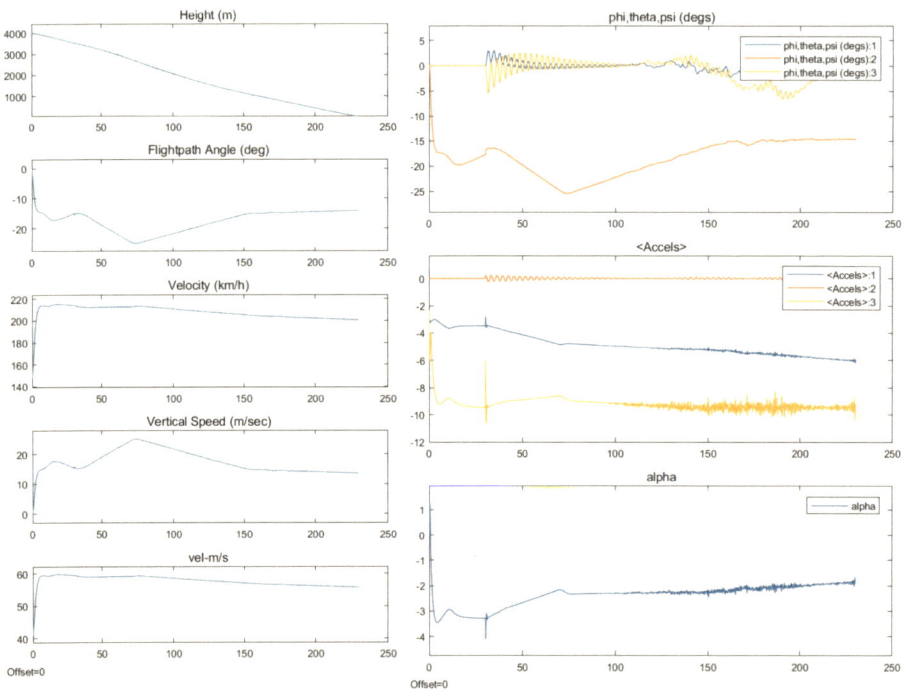

Figure 18.
Topology 1 with turbulence.

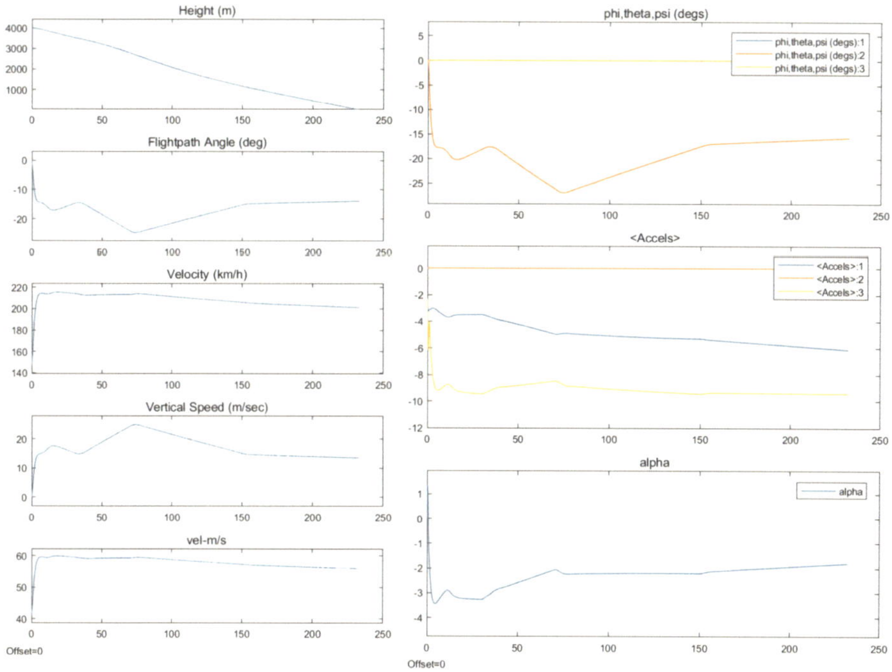

Figure 19.
Topology 1 without turbulence.

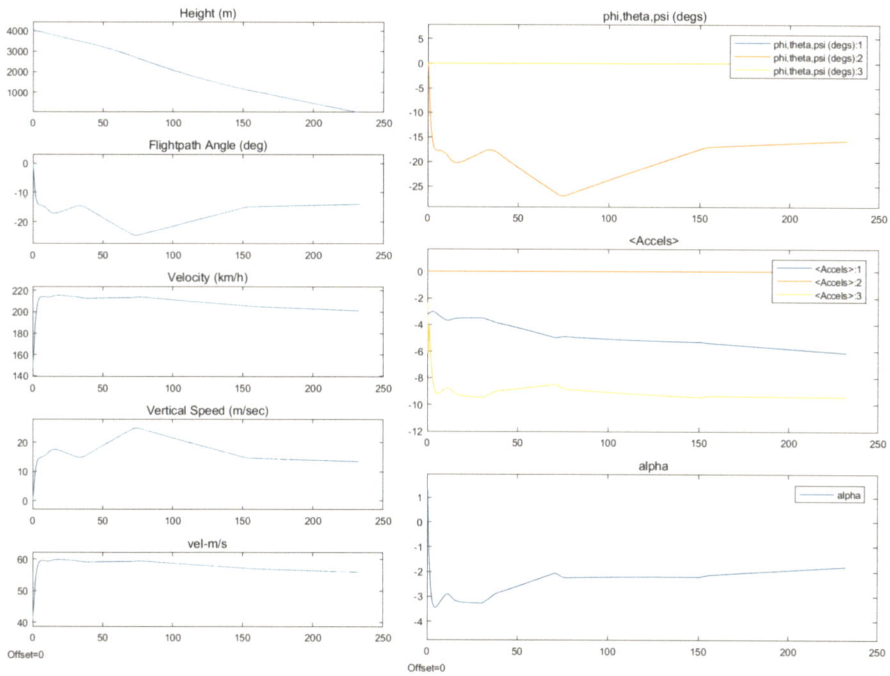

Figure 20.
Topology 2 without turbulence.

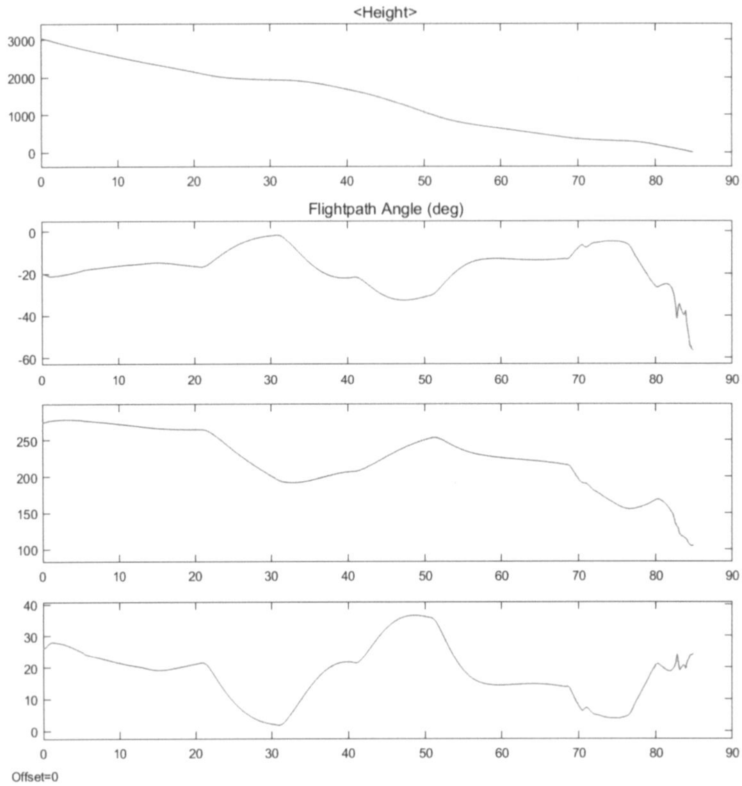

Figure 21.
Topology 2 with a different phase-lead transfer function instead of first-order system.

- Topology 1 without turbulence—**Figure 19**
- Topology 2 with turbulence—**Figure 20**
- Topology 2 without turbulence—**Figure 21**
- Topology 2 with different phase-lead transfer function instead of first-order system—**Figure 21**
- Topology 2 with turbulence and phase-lead transfer function—**Figure 22**.

The phase-lead compensator (instead of first-order compensator) is used in MBC of Topology 2 to reduce the oscillations in the lateral channel and to reduce settling time as a general P + D controller [21, 22]. This compensator improves the transient response by lowering the maximum overshoot and the rise time. The parameters of both compensators have not been included explicitly in the tuning procedure, but they shaped the transient response, which was evaluated by the "best parameter set" choice.

$$G_{MBC}(s) = \frac{s + 1/T_a}{s + \left(\frac{1}{k_a}\right)T_a}$$

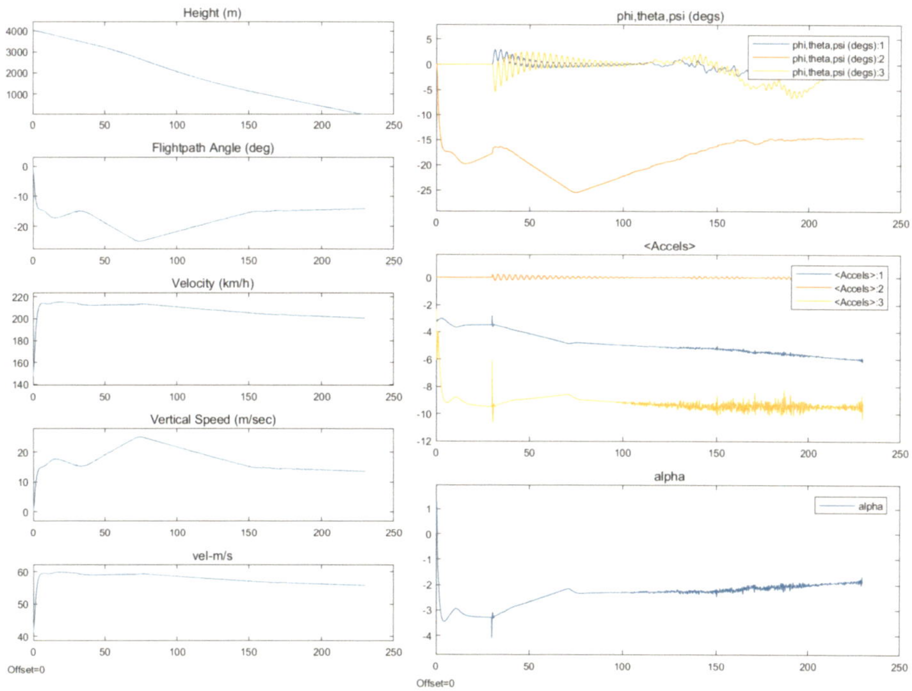

Figure 22.
Topology 2 with turbulence and phase-lead transfer function.

The phase-lead compensator in MBC in many observed responses of closed-loop system generated small and steady oscillations without turbulence. The settling time was a little bit shorter than the usual one. The switching coefficients of sliding mode control of second or first-order are determined from stability conditions of closed-loop systems, using the Lyapunov theorem. The sufficient condition for asymptotic stability of the control system is the Lyapunov function derivative to be negative. The reference system of MBC is a first-order system, so happily the set of calculated gains met the requirements for sliding mode control.

Again, the response of all topologies discussed here is very similar from a closed-loop system view.

MBC demonstrated high robustness as it can cover the entire nonlinear flight dynamics and utilize 5x1 look-up tables for the gains. Even simple gains have been sufficient for altitudes ranging from 4000 m to 0 m. The procedures for tuning the FLCS must be run multiple times to explore the differences between specific sets of gains at different altitudes, angles of attack, and velocities. The differences between sets are within the range of 8%, with the quality of the transition process being more significant. The set of calculated MBC parameters for 2000 m altitude and medium velocity was used for low-altitude flights, and the quality of the transition processes remained similar. The average closest vicinity to the target at a distance of 100 m was ±3.0 m from the Direction of Arrival. The research focuses on 2-loop MBC, but 3-loop MBC was also tested. While this method takes more time to shape the gains, it provides greater possibilities, enhancing the accuracy and complexity of the desired behavior.

6. Discussion

The novel method of deploying the 6D trajectory and model-based control allows guiding a small, subsonic, full-scale tandem test bed platform that meets the requirements. The demonstrator was manufactured, and some real flights were completed. The configurations of AHRS and FLCS required several STM32H750 processors. The flight behavior of the demonstrator was compared to simulations, showing an 85% level of similarity. The outcomes were satisfactory, allowing for the consideration of complex behaviors. Flight logs during turbulence of roll, pitch, azimuth, and flight path angle were very stable and confirmed the simulation results. The joint simulation model results were highly dependent on the correct functioning of the aerodynamics, AHRS, FLCS, and guidance due to oscillations in the roll, pitch, and yaw generated by the vehicle. With appropriately chosen guidance, this problem was resolved. Partial flight log data compared to the proposed model showed that the model accurately replicates the true flight dynamics. Adding appropriate white noise to the radiation seeker changed the performance.

The MBC compensator parameters will be included in the tuning procedure of MBC. Of particular interest is the phase-lead compensator, which generated some promising and stable oscillations observed multiple times in closed-loop system responses. It will be interesting to combine the design of sliding mode control with model-based control. Another feature of interest is the ability of the proposed control strategy to govern systems with non-minimal phase behavior, which is not uncommon in smart munitions.

Future research will investigate the following features:

- Adding a precise model of the radiation seeker to the joint simulation, as well as models of radiation-emitting targets.
- Investigating high angles of diving with different sets of control surfaces.
- Considering the accuracy of the AHRS system as one of the main fidelity factors affecting the entire behavior of the demonstrator.
- Further developing the combination of 3-loop autopilot and MBC.
- Refining the conditions for using the gain-scheduled approach in tuning MBC.
- Carefully investigating the set of control surfaces, as the elevons showed good performance.

The cost-effectiveness enables autonomous UAVs to address complex tasks. A truly cost-effective autonomous platform should not compromise performance.

Author details

Valentin Penev
Institute of Mechanics, Bulgarian Academy of Sciences, Sofia, Bulgaria

*Address all correspondence to: v.penev@imbm.bas.bg

References

[1] Petovello MG. Real-time integration of a tactical-grade IMU and GPS for high-accuracy positioning and navigation [Ph.D. thesis]. Canada: The University of Calgary; 2003

[2] Penev V. Flight dynamics and model based control for fixed wing UAV demonstrator. In: 9th European Conference for Aeronautics and Space Sciences (EUCASS). DOI: 10.13009/EUCASS2022-4660

[3] Penev V. Tandem UAV with inverse dynamics control. Journal of Informatics and Innovative Technologies (JIIT). 2022;**1**:27-40

[4] Penev V. Design and performance of demonstrator of autonomous fixed wing UAV CATLTR. Journal of Theoretical and Applied Mechanics. October 2021;**52** (3):277-293. Print ISSN: 0861-6663

[5] Penev V, Rowlands G, Georgiev G. Novel approach for multi-layered and redundant AHRS in spin stabilized munition. In: 13th National Congress on Theoretical and Applied Mechanics Sofia, Bulgaria, 6-10th September 2017

[6] Mracek C, Ridgely B. Missile Longitudinal Autopilots: Comparison of Multiple Three Loop Topologies, Session: GNC-63: Missile Autopilots. Published Online: June 2012. DOI: 10.2514/6.2005-6380

[7] Blajer W, Goszczyński JA, Krawczyk M. The Inverse Simulation Study of Aircraft Flight Path Reconstruction. DOI: 10.3846/16483840.2002.10414022

[8] Gebre-Egziabher D, Hayward R, Powell J. Design of Multi-sensor Attitude Determination Systems. Aerospace and Electronic Systems, IEEE Transactions. 2004;**40**(2):627-649

[9] Stengel RF. Flight Dynamics. Princeton: Princeton University Press; 2004

[10] Arifianto O, Farhood M. Development and modeling of a low-cost unmanned aerial vehicle research platform. Journal of Intelligent & Robotic Systems. 2015;**80**:139-164

[11] Zhang M, Rizzi A, Meng P, Nangia R, Amiree R, Amoignon O. Aerodynamic design considerations and shape optimization of flying wing in transonic flight. In: Proceedings of the 12th AIAA Aviation Technology, Integration and Operations (ATIO) Conference and 14th AIAA/ISSM, Indianapolis, IN, USA, 17–19 September 2012. pp. 1-17. DOI: 10.2514/6.2012-5402

[12] ANSYS. ANSYS User Manual CFX-Solver Theory Guide. Canonsburg, PA, USA: ANSYS; 2012

[13] Penev V, Rowlands GR, Georgiev GL. Low-cost robust high performance remotely piloted autonomous fixed-wing system. International Journal of Unmanned Systems Engineering (IJUSEng). 2016. ISSN:2052-112X;**4**(1):23-36

[14] Caughey DA. Introduction to Aircraft Stability and Control, Course Notes for Mechanical & Aerospace Engineering. New York, USA: Cornell University; 2011

[15] Ali J, Salman SA, Sreenatha AG, Choi JY. Attitude dynamics identification of unmanned aircraft vehicle. International Journal of Control Automation and Systems. 2006;(1):782-787

[16] Jiang C, Xue L, Chang H, Yuan G, Yuan W. Signal processing of MEMS gyroscope arrays to improve accuracy using a 1st order Markov for rate signal modeling. Sensors. 2012;**12**:1720-1737

[17] Zhang K. Sensing and Control of Mems Accelerometers Using Kalman Filter. China: East China Normal University; 2000

[18] Sargeant MA, Hynes TP, Graham WR. Stability of hybrid-wing-body-type aircraft with centerbody leading-edge carving. Journal of Aircraft. 2010;**47**: 970-974. [CrossRef] Jamson, A.; Schmidt, W.; Turkel, E. Numerical solutions of the Euler equations by finite volume methods using Runge-Kuttatime-stepping schemes. In Proceedings of the 14th Fluid and Plasma Dynamics Conference, Palo Alto, CA, USA, 23–25 June 1981

[19] Jackson EB, Cruz CL. Preliminary subsonic aerodynamic model for simulation studies of the HL-20 lifting body. NASA TM4302. 1992

[20] Karas O. UAV Simulation Environment for Autonomous Flight Control Algorithms. West Virginia University; 2012

[21] Fiorentini L, Serrani A, Doman D. Nonlinear Control of Non-minimum Phase Hypersonic Vehicle Models. IEEE; 2009. DOI: 10.1109/ACC.2009.5160211. Corpus ID: 33136791

[22] Oppenheimer M, Doman D. Control of an unstable, non-minimum phase hypersonic vehicle model mathematics. In: 2006 IEEE Aerospace Conference. DOI: 10.1109/AERO.2006.1655985. Corpus ID: 2467024 2006

Chapter 4

Improving Sustainable Mobility through Intelligent Transport Systems Deployment

Christina Nikolova

Abstract

The following chapter focuses on the contribution of intelligent transport systems to sustainable mobility and the benefits they provide for society. It provides specific examples of intelligent transport systems and their impact on transport sustainability. The chapter also examines the economic implications of intelligent transport systems, discussing how these technologies can reduce external costs related to transportation, such as environmental damage and congestion. Additionally, it delves into the potential cost savings for individuals and governments resulting from the implementation of intelligent transport systems. The author proposes a framework that presents a fresh perspective on the existing theory by adopting a holistic socio-economic approach that considers established methodologies for estimating the external costs of transport in cost-benefit analysis. This approach enhances transparency and provides thorough justification for effective strategies in implementing intelligent transport systems.

Keywords: sustainable mobility, intelligent transport systems, impact assessment, cost-benefit analysis, transport policy

1. Introduction

Intelligent transport systems (ITS) are crucial for promoting sustainable transport and mobility. They help improve transport safety, enhance transport efficiency and infrastructure management, make different modes of transport more environmentally friendly, and ensure smooth transport operations [1]. The impact of intelligent transport systems on sustainable mobility can be framed within various perspectives that cover environmental, social, economic, and technological dimensions.

ITS deployment can optimise traffic flow, reduce congestion, and promote eco-driving, significantly reducing fuel consumption and greenhouse gas emissions. The implementation of intelligent transport systems aligns with sustainable mobility goals by minimising transportation systems' environmental footprint. On the other hand, by integrating ITS with public transport, cycling, and walking infrastructure, cities can encourage a modal shift from private cars to more sustainable forms of transport, further contributing to environmental sustainability [2].

Integrating ITS in existing urban and interurban transportation systems can improve accessibility to transport services for all demographic groups, including the elderly and disabled. By making transportation more efficient and affordable, ITS promotes social equity and inclusion, which are essential components of sustainable mobility [3]. Furthermore, by utilising technologies such as real-time traffic monitoring, collision avoidance systems, and emergency response coordination, ITS can significantly reduce the number of accidents and fatalities, enhancing the overall safety of the transport system.

Regarding optimising infrastructure utilisation, ITS can maximise the efficiency of existing transport infrastructure by managing traffic demand, reducing the need for costly new infrastructure investments, and promoting the optimal use of resources [4]. This contributes to the economic sustainability of transport systems. Moreover, efficient transport systems enabled by ITS deployment can reduce travel time, enhance productivity, and support economic activities, thereby contributing to the economic development of cities and regions. Sustainable mobility, therefore, becomes a driver of broader economic benefits.

In terms of innovation and adaptability, ITS embodies technological innovation that can continuously adapt to changing demands and challenges in urban mobility. This adaptability is crucial for maintaining the long-term sustainability of transport systems, as it allows for the integration of new technologies and practices as they emerge. Something more, ITS provides a wealth of data that can be used to make informed decisions about transport planning, policy-making, and operational adjustments. This evidence-based approach ensures that sustainability goals are effectively met [5].

ITS can be integrated into broader urban planning strategies to create smart cities where transport systems are seamlessly connected with land use, energy, and environmental policies [6]. This holistic approach ensures that mobility solutions contribute to the overall sustainability of urban areas [7]. ITS deployments support policy implementation: they can facilitate the enforcement of policies aimed at reducing car usage, such as congestion pricing or low-emission zones, by providing the necessary technological infrastructure for monitoring and compliance.

By providing real-time information and incentives, ITS can encourage individuals to make more sustainable travel choices, such as using public transportation, carpooling, or cycling [8]. Understanding and influencing travel behaviour is key to achieving sustainable mobility. ITS can also raise public awareness about the environmental and social impacts of different transportation modes, thereby promoting a culture of sustainability.

The scientific rationale for studying the impact of intelligent transport systems on sustainable mobility is rooted in a multidisciplinary approach that spans environmental, social, economic, technological, and policy-related considerations [9]. ITS offers a promising pathway to enhance the sustainability of transport systems by addressing key challenges and leveraging technological advancements to create more efficient, equitable, and environmentally friendly mobility solutions.

2. Scientific context and relevance

The widespread adoption of ITS in the EU is expected to have many positive effects. However, there are also several problems with their deployment. The deployment of ITS in the EU is slow and fragmented at the national level, resulting in uncoordinated solutions at the national, regional, and local levels. There is also inefficiency in addressing urban transport problems. For instance, congestion costs make up around 1% of the EU's GDP, and 71.7% of CO_2 emissions are attributable to transport and continue to rise. Although the number of road deaths is decreasing, further action is necessary to achieve the goals of the European Green Deal. Therefore, it is crucial to conduct an adequate economic assessment to justify the benefits of implementing relevant legislation and introducing ITS for sustainable mobility.

Urbanisation and the increasing demand for mobility have led to significant challenges such as traffic congestion, pollution, and inequitable access to transportation. As cities strive to meet sustainability goals, the need for smarter, more efficient transport systems has become critical. With regard to this, the deployment of ITS offers technological solutions that can optimise traffic flow, enhance public transport, and reduce environmental impact [10]. These systems include advanced traffic management, real-time information systems, and smart infrastructure that support sustainable mobility. However, while substantial research has been conducted on the individual components of ITS, there is a lack of comprehensive studies that analyse the broader impact of ITS on sustainable mobility. Specifically, the interconnections between ITS, environmental outcomes, social equity, and economic efficiency are poorly understood [11].

Existing research often focuses on ITS's short-term or localised impacts. To understand ITS's varying impacts on sustainable mobility, longitudinal studies that assess the long-term effects and comparative studies across different regions or cities are needed [12].

This research can provide valuable insights for policymakers and urban planners by highlighting how intelligent transport systems can be integrated into sustainable urban mobility strategies using a multidimensional holistic approach. The findings could guide ITS investments and develop policies promoting sustainable transportation. By exploring how ITS deployment can contribute to reducing emissions, improving safety, and enhancing the energy efficiency of transportation services, this research can help advance the broader agenda of sustainable mobility in urban and interurban areas.

The study aims to evaluate the effectiveness of ITS projects in promoting sustainable mobility, identify the most impactful ITS components, explore the long-term sustainability outcomes of ITS implementation, and provide recommendations for integrating ITS into sustainable transport policies. This research will contribute to the academic literature on sustainable mobility by providing a holistic understanding of the role of ITS. It will also contribute to technology adoption and innovation theories in urban transport systems. The findings will offer practical guidance for implementing ITS as part of sustainable mobility strategies. By identifying best practices and potential pitfalls, the research can inform the more effective deployment of ITS technologies. This research adopts an interdisciplinary approach, integrating perspectives from urban planning, environmental science, economics, and information technology to analyse the impact of ITS comprehensively.

The study employs advanced data analytics and simulation models to assess the impact of ITS on various dimensions of sustainable mobility, providing robust and actionable insights.

Given the growing challenges of urbanisation and the global emphasis on sustainability, this research is both timely and essential. Understanding the impact of ITS on sustainable mobility can contribute to creating smarter, greener, and more inclusive cities. The outcomes of this study pave the way for further research on the integration of emerging technologies for sustainable mobility.

3. Effects of implementing intelligent transport systems on sustainable mobility

Implementing intelligent transport systems and adopting Directive 2010/40/EU of 7 July 2010 have resulted in both direct and indirect impacts. These impacts have been documented in various studies [13, 14]. *The direct impacts* are linked to increasing interoperability and service continuity with ITS, improving stakeholder cooperation, and clarifying privacy and data collection responsibilities. *Indirect impacts* include the following:

- Economic impacts: These relate to reducing road congestion and associated external costs and increasing carriers' competitiveness. Additionally, users' satisfaction with transport services is higher, and the implementation of ITS deployment projects can lead to economic growth.

- Social impacts: These concerns include road safety and security, as well as employment creation resulting from ITS deployment and operation.

- Environmental impacts: These encompass reducing harmful impacts on the environment and climate change, improving air quality, reducing noise levels, increasing energy efficiency, and creating more favourable conditions for transport.

The implementation of intelligent transport systems in different EU countries has demonstrated that the achieved impacts vary based on the specific type of systems that are put in place. For example, when an open functional platform for ITS-related (on-board) services is implemented, it helps synchronise actions among traffic and transport stakeholders and leads to cost reduction [15]. On the other hand, cooperation and coordination in Europe for the deployment of ITS has required the establishment of an ITS Committee and a European ITS Advisory Group, which provide advisory functions and prepare opinions for European policy purposes. Creating a pan-European framework for the improved collection, exchange, and integration of road and traffic data expands the capabilities of existing services. It enhances their quality in terms of accuracy, coverage, and completeness. This helps ensure continuity of services across countries and modes of transport, thus increasing the potential for achieving sustainable mobility. Consequently, addressing data privacy issues and the operators' liability regarding the use of this data creates the conditions for broader dissemination of warning systems and a significant reduction in accidents.

Indirect impacts in various areas can result from safety-enhancing applications. For instance, these applications can increase driver concentration, reduce traffic fatalities by 5–15%, and reduce serious injuries by 15–20% due to improved emergency care [16]. Traffic management strategies can enhance road connections with other modes and networks (urban-interurban). Additionally, providing more reliable real-time traffic and travel information offers opportunities for improved route planning, time savings, and better pollution control on sensitive road network sections [17]. Introducing other public sector applications can ensure compliance with legal provisions in the social sphere (rest periods), strict monitoring of transport conditions, internalising external costs through electronic toll collection systems, and ensuring transport security monitoring.

The widespread implementation of intelligent transport systems in Europe is essential for achieving sustainable transport and mobility goals. The anticipated benefits include a 2.5% reduction in congestion, a 7% decrease in the costs associated with road traffic accidents, a 1% decrease in total external costs, and improved cooperation and synchronisation in deploying ITS actions [18].

4. Methodological framework for assessing socio-economic and environmental effects of implementing intelligent transport systems

To assess the impact of intelligent transport systems on sustainable mobility, the author recommends using the matrix in **Table 1**. This matrix includes key indicators for evaluating the sustainability of transport development, focusing on economic, social, and environmental effects. We need to evaluate the degree of impact and change that comes from deploying and using ITS for each of these aspects.

When evaluating the socio-economic impacts of implementing ITS, the primary methods utilised include the following:

- Cost-benefit analysis is applied to evaluate the impacts of intelligent transport system deployment projects on sustainable mobility.
- Cost-effectiveness analysis is essential for defining and prioritising transport policy objectives.
- Multi-factor assessments, used to support decision-making on transport policy.
- Estimating users' willingness to pay to use certain ITS: it is important for direct deployment and estimating the return on investment.

When considering projects to implement intelligent transport systems, it is crucial to carry out the following assessments: technical assessment, user acceptability assessment, traffic impact assessment, environmental assessment, and socio-economic assessment. Various evaluation methods should be used depending on the nature of the projects being assessed [19], including the following:

Economic effects	Social effects	Ecological effects
Reducing congestion	Road safety	Climate change
Competitiveness	Employment	Air and noise pollution
Economic benefits for consumers	Security	Energy efficiency
Economic growth		

Table 1.
Matrix for assessing the impact of ITS on sustainable mobility indicators.

4.1 Cost-benefit analysis

This approach has been employed to assess the effectiveness of automated traffic management systems on highways in the USA [20]. It considers various costs such as system costs (including expenses for roadside facilities, traffic management centres, and physical site construction) and user costs (such as onboard device expenses for lateral control, distance keeping, route navigation, and roadside communication systems). The anticipated benefits primarily revolve around time savings. The findings of this evaluation method indicate that if automated traffic management systems are utilised on highways for 250 days a year, 6 hours a day, the estimated time savings amount to USD 10 per hour.

The assessment of advanced traffic management systems in Canada [21] utilises the same method to evaluate different costs and benefits. The costs considered include capital and operating costs, system maintenance costs, and stranded costs due to revenue reduction. On the other hand, the benefits evaluated include travel time savings, reduction in traffic accidents and fuel consumption, impact on regional economic development, and system reliability. The study found that over a 30-year period, the implementation of advanced traffic management systems resulted in economic benefits of USD 2–3.8 billion, with costs amounting to USD 113 million. This translates to a benefit-cost ratio of 18:1 to 33:1. The assessment revealed that approximately 72% of the benefits were attributed to time savings.

An example of using cost-benefit analysis to assess the impact of ITS is the introduction of universal real-time traffic messaging (UK) [22]. The assessment included the systems' capital, operational, and maintenance costs. The benefits evaluated were reduced unintentional driver diversion, optimal route choice, and reduced operating costs resulting from reduced transport distances on alternative routes. The analysis showed a savings of £68,000 annually compared to a capital cost of £150,000.

The widespread adoption of intelligent transportation systems in the United States is estimated to bring significant benefits. This includes reducing the annual cost to the national economy caused by congestion, traffic accidents, and road confusion, estimated at around 300 billion USD. By implementing ITS, these issues are expected to be reduced by an average of 15–20%, resulting in estimated savings of 45–75 billion USD per year. An analysis conducted in 2011 indicated that the total cost of implementing these systems would be 209 billion USD, and the estimated savings would amount to 91 billion USD [22].

4.2 Cost-effectiveness

This method assesses the impact of intelligent transport systems and their economic effects. It involves estimating the present value of costs for various project phases, choosing different cost elements, and specifying the implementation and execution times for alternative ITS projects. Different elements are ranked in order of importance using relative weights, and scale scores are created for the highest and lowest ranked elements. Finally, a weighted score is calculated for each alternative.

When applying this analysis method to the Los Angeles Vehicle Monitoring and Roadway Communication Project [23], the consultants find that an average operating cost of $8000 per vehicle requires a 0.7% reduction in mileage and a 1.6% reduction in the fleet to justify the investment. Using the cost-effectiveness method to evaluate the impact of ITS allows for comparisons of investment projects across different modes and alternative project management.

When evaluating traffic management systems, it is important to identify the specific advantages, such as increased capacity and operational efficiency, enhanced safety, reduced environmental impact and energy consumption, improved productivity of vehicles and transportation services, greater comfort and convenience for passengers, and better coordination among transportation system operators. For each of these criteria, it is necessary to establish measurable indicators. The benefit-cost method can be used for the assessment of indicators that cannot be precisely quantified [24]. However, it is important to remember that the cost-effectiveness method is subjective and requires ranking the achievable objectives. This involves ranking utility estimates and their relative importance using weights, assigning numerical values and scores to each utility estimate, and ultimately calculating the total utility per dollar or euro resulting from the implementation of the project.

4.3 Assessment of users' willingness to pay for the use of ITS

The estimation of users' willingness to pay for the implementation of intelligent transport systems enables us to assess the impact of ITS on vehicle operation, traffic safety, and the potential network benefits. This is typically done through surveys that study users' willingness to pay for the use of ITS.

The assessment of projects for intelligent transport systems' deployment is crucial for making transport policy decisions at both national and international levels. This type of evaluation relies on established key performance indicators for intelligent transport systems [25]. The widespread implementation of intelligent transport systems and the action plan for their extensive deployment in road transport require better coordination in assessing their impact. Some challenges arise when measuring certain impacts and societal benefits regarding value. Additionally, existing methods for evaluating the socio-economic impact of ITS projects do not comprehensively capture all the system's impacts [26]. Therefore, it is essential to develop a methodology for evaluating ITS deployment projects that align in form, content, and consistency with the methods used for conventional transport infrastructure projects.

5. Impact assessment and application of cost-benefit analysis for evaluating ITS projects

The impact assessment of projects deploying ITS on sustainable mobility aims to evaluate the value of the achieved results in terms of overall well-being. Transport investments have direct or indirect impacts on external parties such as administrative authorities, transport users, business organisations, landowners. Each of these parties is interested in assessing and measuring the impact of ITS projects on their activities. Furthermore, the economic analysis conducted in this context aims to identify the projects' societal benefits in achieving sustainable mobility.

The most commonly used methods for economic evaluation and measuring the effectiveness of investments in transport projects are cost-benefit analysis, which helps in weighing the benefits against the costs; cost-effectiveness analysis, which is crucial for defining and prioritising transport policy objectives; and multi-factor evaluations, which are used to support transport policy decision-making.

Investment decisions can only be truly effective when they are based on the current and future levels of infrastructure provision and intelligent transport systems. These systems should deliver sustainable mobility benefits. Decision-making should involve a comprehensive public cost-benefit analysis that considers all public and private societal costs and benefits. Since benefits may also accrue to those who do not use the respective intelligent transport systems, it would be highly inefficient to suggest that the direct users should bear all costs of each individual investment project. Applying full cost recovery at the individual project level would not only lead to overall inefficiencies in the use of the intelligent transport systems deployed but also distort investment decisions.

It can be challenging to measure the full impact and benefits of ITS projects on society in monetary terms. Current evaluation methods for these projects do not cover all the impacts that ITS can have. Therefore, it is important to concentrate on creating a standard method for assessing the impacts of ITS projects. This method should be consistent and comprehensive, allowing for the evaluation of whether sustainable mobility objectives are being met.

The successful implementation of ITS deployment projects relies heavily on the following crucial assessments: technical assessment, which examines the technological aspects; traffic impact assessment, which evaluates the effects on traffic flow; environmental assessment, which considers the ecological impact; and socio-economic assessment, which analyses the effects on the community and economy.

5.1 Impact assessment and the cost-benefit analysis for projects to implement intelligent transportation systems in Bulgaria

To showcase the effectiveness of cost-benefit analysis in evaluating the influence of implemented ITS projects on sustainable mobility, we utilised data on implementing six ITS projects in various EU countries in 2014. We then updated the information on their performance 10 years later. The projects include the following:

1. Introduction of an advanced travel information system—Advanced Traveller Information Services (ATIS), based on real-time data transmission—the project was implemented in the cities of Patras and Thessaloniki in Greece.

2. Cooperative traffic management system (C-ITS)—collects real-time traffic data and delivers it to end users on mobile devices. It has been piloted in Vienna, Austria.

3. Introduction of bluetooth information system (BTiS)—provides services based on real-time traffic information collected by bluetooth sensors. The collected information covers travel times and a matrix of trip origin and destination points. The system has been implemented in Sofia, Bulgaria

4. The multimodal traveller information (MTI) system provides access to information and travel planning solutions for four different modes of transport by combining traffic and route information for public urban, rail, road, and inland waterway transports. The project has been piloted in Romania

5. Monitoring of the transit of dangerous goods (MTDG). The system is based on the identification of danger signs and the definition of the points and direction of movement of vehicles transporting dangerous goods. The system has been implemented on the Emilia Romana route in Italy

6. Professional route planning engine (PRPE)—Introduced in Budapest, Hungary, PRPE allows the use of public transport timetables, and the calculation of the time required for cycling in the presence of cycle lanes and the time required for walking

The Impact and Benefit Assessment Report of ITS Implementation Projects [27], regarding sustainable mobility aspects, reflects the percentage-based benefits identified by contractors (**Table 2**).

We conduct a transfer of results to evaluate the costs and benefits of ITS projects implemented in other countries based on local conditions. This method is suggested at the EU level when there are no cost and impact data available for the projects in the relevant countries.

When carrying out ITS deployment projects, it is important to consider that there will be an initial investment, and the benefits will accumulate over a significant period of time. Consequently, it is essential to compare the costs and benefits that arise over different time periods. Since the value of money changes over time, it is crucial to convert the relevant cash flows into an equivalent time frame when conducting a cost-benefit analysis.

The cost-benefit analysis framework was developed using the following sequence to estimate the costs and benefits of an ITS project deployment [28]:

5.1.1 Defining the scope of the analysis

The cost-benefit analysis for implementing ITS projects in Bulgaria assesses the project's impact over a seven-year period (from 2024 to 2030). The analysis encompasses the project's costs, including investment, maintenance, and operational expenses.

5.1.2 Estimation of investment costs

Investment costs are usually determined based on engineering decisions and performance estimates. For economic analysis, adjustments have been made to account

Expected benefits at local level (updated for 2024–2030)	**Projects**					
	ATIS	**C-ITS**	**MTI**	**MTDG**	**PRPE**	**BTiS**
1. Travel time savings (car hours)	2200	1162	4932	n.i.	469	319
2. Reducing the number of transport accidents, incl.:						
• deaths (no.)	n.i.	11	n.i.	1	n.i.	n.i.
• serious incidents (no.)	n.i.	22	n.i.	4	n.i.	n.i.
• minor incidents (no.)	n.i.	26	n.i.	n.i.	n.i.	n.i.
• material losses (in €)	n.i.	517,209	n.i.	n.i.	n.i.	n.i.
3. Reduction of CO_2 emissions (tonnes)	5473	1	n.i.	n.i.	n.i.	5
4. Fuel consumption reduction (litres)	15,584	n.i.	1893	n.i.	n.i.	n.i.

Source: SEE-ITS. Deliverable 6.1 and authors' own calculations of updates based on national traffic analysis.
Note: n.i.—Relevant benefits were not identified during the implementation of the project.

Table 2.
Expected benefits from the implementation of ITS in Bulgaria at local level.

for inflation between the year of the engineering estimates (2014) and the subsequent years up to 2030, based on actual market value.

5.1.3 Operation and maintenance costs

The costs of maintaining the ITS infrastructure and providing mode-specific services in each country have been estimated using the same cost categories. The main cost categories are infrastructure operating costs, maintenance costs, and changes in the operating costs of the vehicles used for public transport services. The impact assessment also considers any service disruptions caused by ongoing operations.

5.1.4 Assessment of user benefits and travel time savings

The quantification of the advantages to users resulting from changes in travel durations because of enhancements in transportation conditions and quality considers the time spent by users on journeys and the associated cost. These costs encompass all time expenses that could otherwise be utilised for different activities, as well as the inconvenience experienced when travelling between two points using a specific mode of transportation.

It is important to note that total costs differ depending on the mode of transportation. This results in different benefits for users. Additionally, the value of time varies from person to person, depending on factors such as the purpose of travel. As a result, there is not a standard way to assess the value of travel time savings. Therefore, the cost-benefit analysis framework considers reference values of travel time that are valid for the specific country (for Bulgaria) if those values are defined according to widely accepted methodologies [29].

5.1.5 Safety benefits

The enhancement of transport safety is not considered as part of the general category of other user benefits. Instead of being classified as a component of the fixed costs of transport services, the expenses associated with managing the aftermath of transport accidents are treated as a separate category resulting from the operation of the transport system. The reduction in these costs due to the implementation of intelligent transportation systems projects is estimated based on reference values for accidents or lives lost [29]. The actual benefits are determined by multiplying the decrease in the estimated number of accidents (based on injury rate) by the per-accident reference value. This method is similar to the approach used for calculating external costs, such as those related to protecting the environment from pollution.

External accident costs include direct and indirect economic costs such as medical and rehabilitation costs, insurance system costs, administrative costs, production losses, material damage costs (including country average damage reference values), and safety assessment values [30].

5.1.6 Environmental, noise, and global warming benefits

The investment in intelligent transport systems is expected to bring about significant environmental benefits. When conducting a cost-benefit analysis, the focus is on evaluating externalities such as air pollution, noise, and global warming. The assessment method is used to measure these impacts and aims to uncover the positive effects of implementing ITS projects. The calculation process involves several steps:

- Quantifying the changes (reductions) in pollutant emissions in tonnes, taking into account factors such as regions and people exposed to noise or CO_2 emissions, using current European values for these factors.

- Categorising emissions (noise type) based on regional characteristics, such as urban or suburban areas.

- Adjusting the benchmarks by multiplying them by the GDP per capita growth for each year of the analysis.

- Calculating the benefits by multiplying the emissions by the impact rate (e.g. percentage reduction) and by the reference value of the corresponding cost.

These calculations help determine the degree of impact and cost savings to society.

5.1.7 Calculation of the benefit-cost ratio

The costs and benefits of specific ITS projects are converted into equivalent present values before the benefit-cost assessment is conducted to evaluate the projects. The base year for this assessment is 2024. All investment costs incurred in previous periods have been converted into present values as of the base year, considering the country's inflation growth. Future costs for maintenance and operation, as well as benefits, have also been converted to present values using a standard formula:

$$PV = FV / (1 + \mathrm{r})^{\mathrm{N}} \tag{1}$$

where PV is the present value.

FV—the future value of the benefits or costs involved.

r—discount rate (for transport projects at EU level, a rate of 5.5% has been set), and N—years of project use (usually 5–10 years for ITS projects).

5.1.8 Transfer of results of ITS implementation to other countries

For the purpose of evaluating the costs and benefits of ITS projects conducted in other countries, the results are adjusted to fit Bulgarian conditions. This method has been recommended at the EU level due to the lack of cost and impact data for projects in the respective countries [31]. The costs and benefits for implementing these projects in Bulgaria were calculated based on the recommended costing methods for ITS projects. Additionally, the costs and benefits for the initial implementation of projects in other countries were recalculated for Bulgaria and adjusted to align with the national economic conditions using the ratios between the GDP in purchasing power parity for Bulgaria and the respective country where the project was piloted.

The results of the cost-benefit analysis are summarised in **Table 3**.

The benefit-cost ratio (BCR) demonstrates the value of the benefits realised by users and society due to the introduction of the relevant intelligent transport system

Types of costs and benefits	Cost-benefit figures (in euro) for ITS projects					
	ATIS	C-ITS	MTI	MTDG	PRPE	BTiS
Benefits						
1. Travel time saving	36,355	18,289	81,534	n.i.	7755	5278
2. Reduction in the number of accidents	n.i.	8,871,840	n.i.	493,442	n.i.	n.i.
3. Reduction of CO_2 emissions	165,214	1	n.i.	n.i.	n.i.	140
4. Reduction in fuel consumption	35,631	n.i.	3126	n.i.	n.i.	n.i.
Benefits—total	237,199	8,890,131	84,660	493,442	7755	5418
Costs						
1. Infrastructure costs of the respective system	41,684	27,396	18,879	90,154	43,820	18,220
2. Maintenance and operating costs	17,200	30,645	51,612	126,132	7788	1700
Costs—total	58,884	58,041	70,490	216,285	51,609	19,920
Benefit-cost ratio	4,03	153,17	1,20	2,28	0,15	0,27

Source: SEE-ITS. Deliverable 7.1. and authors' own calculations of updated values.
Note: n.i.—relevant benefits have not been identified for the specific project.

Table 3.
Cost-benefit analysis for each of the ITS implementation projects in Bulgaria.

compared to the project's costs. A higher ratio indicates a more profitable investment in the ITS.

Upon comparing the BCRs of various pilot projects hypothetically implemented in Bulgaria (excluding the already implemented BTiS), it is evident that the project introducing a cooperative traffic management system (C-ITS) stands out as the most profitable. With a benefit-cost ratio of 157.05 EUR, this project yields 157.05 EUR in benefits for every 1 EUR in costs. Consequently, it offers the highest benefits regarding improved sustainable mobility performance.

6. Exploring the potential uses of multi-criteria analysis in assessing the influence of ITS on sustainable mobility

The implementation of intelligent transport systems and the need to evaluate their economic impact are crucial aspects of the strategy for deploying ITS. The widespread use of ITS in Europe is closely tied to achieving sustainable mobility goals. It is expected that ITS implementation will lead to a 2.5% reduction in congestion, a 7% decrease in the cost of managing traffic accidents, a 1% decrease in total external costs, and enhanced cooperation and coordination in deploying ITS actions [31].

An essential component of making informed transport policy decisions to achieve sustainable mobility at both national and international levels is the socio-economic evaluation of projects for the implementation of intelligent transport systems [32]. The widespread development and deployment of these systems necessitate improved coordination in assessing their impact.

Quantifying the societal impacts and benefits of achieving sustainable mobility poses inherent difficulties. Additionally, existing methods for evaluating the socio-economic impacts of ITS projects do not encompass all system impacts. Therefore, it is essential to concentrate on developing a uniform evaluation methodology for ITS deployment projects, ensuring consistency in format and content. This will facilitate an unbiased assessment of ITS impact on sustainable transport and mobility development.

To determine the need for ITS deployment in the country, all proposed project impacts should be compared with the expected development of transport and infrastructure as per the adopted national policy [32].

When evaluating proposed projects, it is crucial to employ a robust methodology such as multi-criteria analysis [33]. This approach allows for a thorough assessment of the effectiveness of the projects, providing preliminary estimates of their potential impacts and outcomes (**Figure 1**). The criteria considered in this type of analysis can encompass various aspects such as cost, time, resources, environmental impact, and stakeholder preferences, among others. By incorporating multiple criteria, a more comprehensive understanding of the potential implications of the projects can be achieved, helping decision-makers make well-informed choices, as follows:

- The project's *direct impacts* on accelerating ITS deployment can be assessed against sustainable mobility criteria. These impacts include the following:
    - Improved interoperability and service continuity
    - Increased coherence and cooperation among stakeholders
    - Resolution of ambiguities related to confidentiality and liability and clear definition of the responsibilities of all project participants
- *Indirect economic, social, and environmental impacts* arising from the implementation of the projects and contributing to the achievement of transport policy objectives such as:

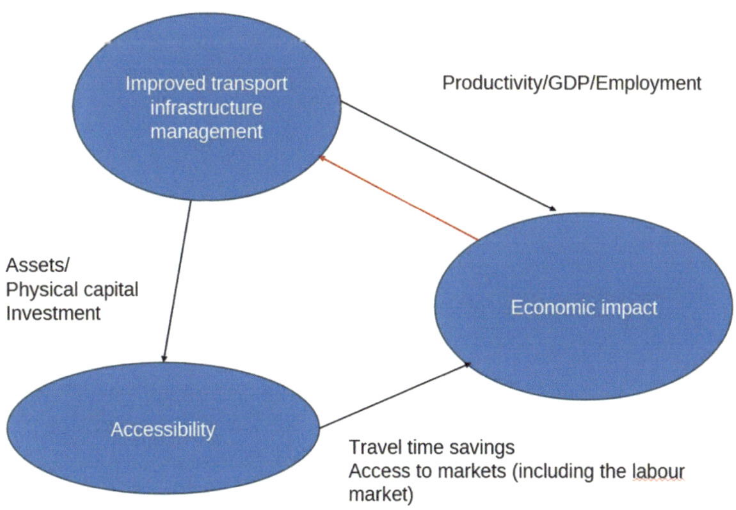

Figure 1.
Elements of the multi-criteria analysis of the impacts of ITS implementation.

- *Economic impacts*: reduction of road congestion, increase in competitiveness (incl. Public transport, costs of implementing systems, innovation), benefits for consumers (prices of services, increase in choices, new service offerings, privacy protection), economic growth.
- *Social impacts*: increased road safety (reduced number of road accidents, reduced number of people killed and injured in road accidents, reduced material damage), employment (creation of new jobs), increased security.
- *Environmental impacts* include the reduction of environmental pollution, such as greenhouse gas and carbon dioxide emissions, as well as particulate matter and nitrogen oxides, measured in tonnes. Energy efficiency is also improved, resulting in reduced fuel consumption measured in litres. Furthermore, objectives related to the provision of intermodality of public transport, such as creating opportunities for smooth transfer of passengers and freight between different modes of transport and changing the ratio between different modes of transport, are fulfilled.

Additionally, we can estimate the total external costs that will be reduced or increased due to the project's implementation to assess its impact on national budget expenditures (see **Figure 2**).

The project's impact assessment can cover short- to medium-term effects (e.g., up to 2030). Longer-term impacts (after 2030) usually stem from increased interest in adopting new technologies, achieving greater market penetration, and influencing the attitudes of transport service users and infrastructure users [34].

The impact assessment cannot cover all aspects and outcomes of project implementation. It aims to show how a project will contribute to achieving the national transport policy objectives related to sustainable mobility and coordinated actions for ITS deployment. An important factor to consider is the time perspective, which determines when positive project results will be achieved.

Fundamentally, each of these assessments is based on qualitative expression, and it is possible to establish an impact scale for each. One way to do this is using the Likert scale [31]. The scale could be as follows: an impact scale can be defined for each of them, for example, on the Likert scale:

- Positive;
- Slightly positive;
- Neutral;
- Slightly negative; and
- Negative.

Many EU-funded research and innovation projects utilise stakeholder interviews, surveys, and external consultant support for evaluation.

The cost-benefit assessment is just a part of the overall evaluation of the impact of ITS deployment projects on sustainable mobility. It does not fully capture all aspects of this impact, some of which are difficult to measure in value terms. Therefore, while cost-benefit analysis is necessary for deciding on the funding of individual

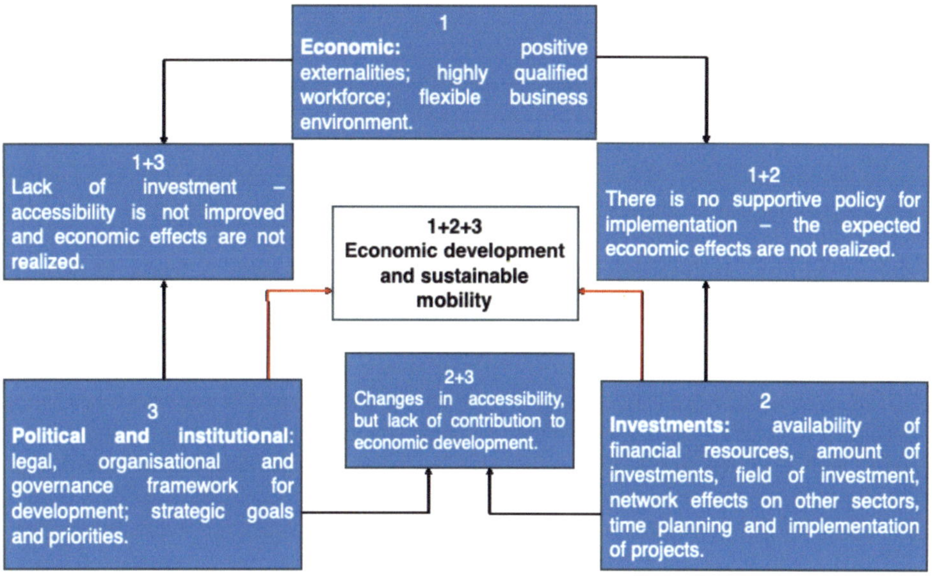

Figure 2.
Key factors for an effective ITS deployment policy and for promoting the development of sustainable mobility.

sustainable mobility projects, additional technical and advisory assistance is required to support the private sector. In the previous section, specific examples have been presented of using benefit-cost ratios to assess projects for the deployment of intelligent transport systems. However, this approach does not provide a complete and accurate assessment of the sustainability impacts of implementing these systems [35].

The proposed methodological framework for evaluating project proposals for ITS implementation is primarily concerned with establishing selection criteria and prioritising project proposals. Additionally, it aims to align the selection of projects for funding with priority areas for ITS development and assess their potential contribution to strengthening cooperation. Quantitative evaluations, including transport market analysis, demand forecasts, and traffic simulations, can enhance the impact assessments of individual projects on sustainable mobility.

When establishing the framework for the multi-criteria analysis, it is important to bear in mind that the proven benefits of ITS deployment, such as decreased congestion, lower fuel consumption and costs, and enhanced transport reliability and safety, will enhance the appeal of transportation activity and driving. Consequently, this will lead to increased demand for transport, resulting in induced traffic. Therefore, an escalation in the volume of transport activity (in tonne-kilometres or passenger-kilometres) may impede the realisation of certain benefits associated with implementing the systems to achieve sustainable mobility objectives.

7. Conclusions

Intelligent transport systems have varying levels of popularity and adoption across different countries. The main reason for investing in ITS is to enhance transport operations, ensure sustainable mobility, and achieve benefits such as increased productivity, saved lives, and reduced time, cost, and energy. The term ITS is flexible and can be broadly or narrowly interpreted. ITS' main function is to improve real-time decision-making, thereby enhancing the entire transport system and promoting sustainability in mobility development. In the upcoming decades, society, the transport sector, and world economies will increasingly rely on ITS, often without being fully aware of it.

Intelligent transport systems use telecommunications, electronic, and information technologies in combination with transport engineering to plan, design, operate, and manage transport systems. The use of information and communication technologies in the transport sector is expected to significantly improve environmental performance and efficiency, including energy efficiency, safety and security of transport, and mobility of passengers and freight. This will also ensure the functioning of the EU internal market and contribute to a higher level of competitiveness and employment, leading to increased sustainability of transport and the EU economy as a whole.

ITS and related technologies have wide applications in both the public and private sectors. They are designed to ensure that the goal of sustainable mobility is achieved while contributing to an improved quality of life. However, the road to widespread deployment of these systems is not without its challenges. Many of the technologies used have been proven effective, but the more difficult issues are those related to solving social, institutional, and political problems. All of this requires a precise assessment of these systems' contribution to achieving sustainable transport objectives. In this context, the research and analyses carried out show that the application of standard methods for analysing and evaluating the impact of ITS deployment projects does not fully clarify their impact on sustainable mobility. To address this, the author justifies the application of multi-criteria analysis, which covers all major aspects of transport system sustainability and thus creates opportunities to accurately assess the impact of ITS on sustainable development indicators.

Funding

The Bulgarian National Scientific Research Fund has funded this research, grant number KP-06-N55/15 of 22.11.2021.

Author details

Christina Nikolova
University of National and World Economy, Sofia, Bulgaria

*Address all correspondence to: hrnikolova@unwe.bg

References

[1] European Commission. Sustainable and Smart Mobility Strategy—Putting European Transport on Track for the Future. Mobility and Transport [Online] 2023. Available from: https://transport.ec.europa.eu/news-events/news/sustainable-transport-rules-boost-intelligent-transport-systems-safer-and-more-efficient-transport-2023-06-09_en [Accessed: July 20, 2024]

[2] Banister D. The sustainable mobility paradigm. Transport Policy. 2008;**15**(2):73-80. Available from: https://www.sciencedirect.com/science/article/abs/pii/S0967070X07000820 [Accessed: July 20, 2024]

[3] Newman P, Kenworthy J. Sustainability and Cities: Overcoming Automobile Dependence. Washington: Island Press; 2013

[4] Hickman R, Banister D. Transport, Climate Change and the City. London, New York: Routledge; 2014

[5] Geels FW. A socio-technical analysis of low-carbon transitions: Introducing the multi-level perspective into transport studies. Journal of Transport Geography. 2012;**24**:471-482. Available from: https://www.sciencedirect.com/science/article/abs/pii/S0966692312000269 [Accessed: July 21, 2024]

[6] Litman T. The new transportation planning paradigm. ITE Journal. 2013;**83**(6):20-28. Available from: https://www.vtpi.org/paradigm.pdf [Accessed: July 21, 2024]

[7] Alessandrini A, Site PD, Filippi F. A new planning paradigm for urban sustainability. Transportation Research Procedia. 2023;**69**:203-210. DOI: 10.1016/j.trpro.2023.02.163 [Accessed: July 22, 2024]

[8] Zhang X, Qi S, Zheng A, Luo Y, Hao S. Data-driven analysis of fatal urban traffic accident characteristics and safety enhancement research. Sustainability. 2023;**15**(4):3259. DOI: 10.3390/su15043259 [Accessed: July 23, 2024]

[9] Marsden G, Reardon L. Questions of governance: Rethinking the study of transportation policy. Transportation Research Part A: Policy and Practice. 2018;**101**:238-251. DOI: 10.1016/j.tra.2017.05.008 [Accessed: July 23, 2024]

[10] Stawiarska E, Sobczak P. The impact of intelligent transportation system implementations on the sustainable growth of passenger transport in EU regions. Sustainability. 2018;**10**(5):1318. DOI: 10.3390/su10051318 [Accessed: July 23, 2024]

[11] Badi M, Bouraima B, Muhammad LJ. The role of intelligent transportation systems in solving traffic problems and reducing environmental negative impact of urban transport. Decision Making and Analysis. 2022;**1**(1):1-9. Available from: https://www.mendeley.com/catalogue/4d0cf088-60f7-3e81-91e9-e7829b480ed8/ [Accessed: July 23, 2023]

[12] Elassy M, Al-Hattab M, Takruri M, Badawi S. Intelligent transportation systems for sustainable smart cities. Transportation Engineering. 2024;**16**:100252. DOI: 10.1016/j.treng.2024.100252 [Accessed: July 24, 2024]

[13] European Commission. Directive 2010/40/EU on the framework for the deployment of Intelligent Transport

Systems in the field of road transport and for interfaces with other modes of transport. Transport and Mobility. [Online] 2023. Available from: https://eur-lex.europa.eu/legal-content/en/TXT/?uri=CELEX%3A32023L2661 [Accessed: June 28, 2024]

[14] DG MOVE. Intelligent Transport Systems in Action. Brussels: Directorate General for Mobility and Transport; 2023. Available from: https://transport.ec.europa.eu/transport-themes/intelligent-transport-systems/road/its-directive-and-action-plan_en [Accessed: June 26 2024]

[15] DG TREN. Intelligent Transport Systems: A Smart Move for Europe. Brussels: Directorate General for Energy and Transport, European Communities; 2009

[16] European Commission: Directorate-General for Mobility and Transport, Tsamis A, Gibson G, Biedka M, Löhr E, et al. Support Study for the Ex-post Evaluation of the ITS Directive 2010/40/EU – Final Report. Brussels: Publications Office of the European Union; 2019. Available from: https://data.europa.eu/doi/10.2832/254167 [Accessed: June 26, 2024]

[17] Zhang X, Shaheen S, Chen X. Understanding ridesplitting behavior of on-demand ride services: An ensemble learning approach. Transportation Research Part C: Emerging Technologies. 2017;**76**:51-70. Available from: https://www.sciencedirect.com/science/article/abs/pii/S0968090X16302728 [Accessed: June 17, 2024]

[18] European Commission. Intelligent Transport Systems: EU-Funded Research for Efficient, Clean and Safe Road Transport. Luxembourg: Directorate-General for Research and Innovation: Transport; 2012

[19] Zhicai J, Jianping W, McDonald M. Socio-economic impact assessment of intelligent transport systems. Tsinghua Science and Technology. 2006;**6**:339-350

[20] Lee K, Ran B, Dong H. Cost-benefit analysis on deployment of automated highway systems. Transportation Research Record. 1997;**1588**:137-144

[21] Schnarr TJ, Kitaska K. Evaluating ATMS from a Business Respective: Vancouver's Traffic Management Program. Orlando: Third World Congress in Intelligent Transportation Systems; 1996

[22] Tarry S, Graham A. The role of valuation in ATT development (part 4): Evaluation of ATT systems. Traffic Engineering & Control. 1995;**36**(12):688-693

[23] Harvey S. The political and economic implications of ATT: Towards an intelligent transport system. In: Proceedings of the 1st World Congress on Applications of Transport Telematics and Intelligent Vehicle-Highway Systems. Vol. 6. Boston: Artech House; 1994. pp. 3125-3132

[24] Daetz D, Bebendorf M. A Socio-Economic Impact Assessment of the Los Angeles Automatic Vehicle Monitoring (AVM) Demonstration. Washington, DC: SYSTAN Incorporated, Urban Mass Transportation Administration; 1982

[25] AECOM. Key Performance Indicators for Intelligent Transport Systems—Final Report. Brussels: European Commission; 2015. Available from: https://transport.ec.europa.eu/document/download/6e679027-4827-48a3-8482-418bd486a6f6_en?filename=its-kpi-final_report_v7_4.pdf [Accessed: October 15, 2023]

[26] Quinet E, Vickerman R. Principles of Transport Economics. London: Edward Elgar Publishing; 2004. p. 2581

[27] SEE-ITS. Deliverable 6.1. Impact Assessment Studies of Cooperative ITS Applications in SEE Countries at the Regional Level. Brussels: SEE-ITS; 2014

[28] Nikolova C. Deliverable 7.1. Cost-Benefit Analysis Report for the Deployment of ITS in Bulgaria. SEE-ITS. Sofia: SEE-ITS; 2015

[29] European Commission, Directorate-general for mobility and transport, Essen H, Fiorello D, El Beyrouty K, et al. Handbook on the External Costs of Transport—Version 2019-1.1, Publications Office 2020. Available from: https://data.europa.eu/doi/10.2832/51388 [Accessed: October 10, 2023]

[30] Schoeters A, Wijnen W, Carnis L, Weijermars W, Elvik R, Johannsen H, et al. Costs Related to Serious Injuries, D7.3 of the H2020 Project SafetyCube. 2017. Available from: https://www.safetycube-project.eu/wp-content/uploads/SafetyCube-D7.3-Costs-related-to-serious-road-injuries.pdf [Accessed: July 25, 2024]

[31] Web Center for Social Research Methods. Research Methods Knowledge Base: Liker Scaling. 2016. Available from: http://www.socialresearchmethods.net/kb/scallik.php [Accessed: October 23, 2023]

[32] Zhou J. Sustainable transportation in the US: A review of proposals, policies, and programs since 2000. Frontiers of Architectural Research. 2012;**1**(2):150-165. DOI: 10.1016/j.foar.2012.02.012 [Accessed: August 9, 2024]

[33] Grant-Muller S, Kolosz B. Sustainability assessment approaches for intelligent transport systems: The state of the art. IET Intelligent Transport Systems. 2016;**10**(5):287-297. DOI: 10.1049/iet-its.2015.0025 [Accessed: August 9, 2024]

[34] Giannoutakis KN, Li F. Making a business case for intelligent transport systems: A holistic business model framework. Transport Reviews. 2012;**32**(6):781-804. DOI: 10.1080/01441647.2012.740096 [Accessed: June 25, 2024]

[35] Yan J, Liu J, Tseng F-M. An evaluation system based on the self-organizing system framework of smart cities: A case study of smart transportation systems in China. Technological Forecasting and Social Change. 2020;**153**:11937. DOI: 10.1016/j.techfore.2018.07.009 [Accessed: August 9, 2024]

Chapter 5

Deep Learning for Planning and Control in Autonomous Vehicles

Jingyuan Zhao and Andrew F. Burke

Abstract

In autonomous systems, path planning and control are critical for ensuring safety, efficiency, and comfort. Deep learning has significantly enhanced these aspects by introducing adaptability and real-time responsiveness into autonomous operations. Reinforcement learning-based motion planning algorithms, for example, are adept at devising optimal navigation paths even within intricate environments. Moreover, trajectory prediction models, particularly those employing recurrent neural networks, excel in anticipating the movements of nearby objects accurately. Furthermore, the integration of end-to-end methodologies has augmented the capabilities of autonomous control systems, providing a more streamlined approach to decision-making processes. The application of explainable AI techniques brings a layer of transparency to these technologies, elucidating the reasoning behind decisions and fostering trust among users. Herein, we explore these technological advancements and examine their impact on the development of autonomous vehicle technology.

Keywords: autonomous driving, motion planning, trajectory prediction, decision-making, artificial intelligence, deep learning, neural networks, end-to-end, explainable AI

1. Introduction

Once an autonomous vehicle has perceived its environment and formulated high-level strategic decisions, the essential stages of planning and control commence (**Figure 1**). These stages involve defining a safe, efficient, and comfortable trajectory while executing the precise maneuvers needed to follow this path [1, 2]. The transformative role of deep learning in these processes has introduced unprecedented adaptability and responsiveness [3, 4], addressing the growing need for autonomous vehicles to navigate complex and dynamic environments in real time. As summarized in **Table 1**, advancements in reinforcement learning, trajectory prediction, and end-to-end control are at the forefront of these developments, each tackling specific objectives and challenges within autonomous vehicle technology.

Reinforcement learning algorithms have proven highly effective for motion planning, enabling autonomous vehicles to optimize action sequences to ensure safe navigation in diverse scenarios [5]. Trajectory prediction [6], crucial for anticipating the movement of

Figure 1.
Motion planning in autonomous driving.

Research	Deep learning	Goals	Challenges
Reinforcement learning for motion planning	DDPG, PPO, A3C, DQN	Enable vehicles to learn optimal action sequences for safe navigation	Reward design, exploration, real-time planning
Deep learning-based trajectory prediction for path planning	LSTM, CNN, attention mechanisms	Predict future trajectories of dynamic objects for effective planning	Uncertainty modeling, long-range prediction, complex scenarios
End-to-end learning for autonomous vehicle control	CNNs, DNNs	Develop models that directly map sensor inputs to control actions	Latency, safety guarantees, lack of interpretability

Table 1.
Overview of planning and control research: Techniques, objectives, and challenges.

surrounding objects, leverages models such as recurrent neural networks (RNNs) and attention mechanisms to make accurate forecasts, enhancing the ability to plan preemptively. Deep learning-based end-to-end approaches have further simplified the control process by mapping sensor inputs directly to control actions, reducing latency and operational complexity [7]. However, these advancements come with unique challenges. Issues such as reward design and real-time adaptation in RL, uncertainty modeling in trajectory prediction, and interpretability in end-to-end control continue to shape the research landscape. To address interpretability, the integration of explainable AI (XAI) methods is increasingly common, aiming to foster transparency and trust in decision-making processes. This section provides an in-depth analysis of these technological innovations, highlighting how deep learning is reshaping autonomous planning and control and discussing its broader implications for autonomous vehicle technology.

1.1 Reinforcement learning for motion planning

Reinforcement learning for motion planning is critical in autonomous driving due to its pivotal role in optimizing navigation strategies. This section reviews the advancements in deep learning, specifically the application of RL in the context of motion planning (**Figure 1**), where it enables vehicles to learn and refine their trajectories through trial and error in simulated environments. By continuously interacting with a dynamic environment, RL can develop policies that not only ensure safety and efficiency but also adapt to changing traffic conditions and unforeseen obstacles. This adaptive capacity is crucial for autonomous vehicles that must navigate complex urban landscapes.

The field of RL in the context of motion planning for autonomous driving is rapidly evolving, with each study shedding light on different intricate challenges. For instance, one study proposed a conditional deep Q-network (CDQN) method, employing fuzzy logic to smooth out wrinkles in directional planning for autonomous driving systems [8]. The CDQN consists of two key parts: a state encoder network and a policy network. The state encoder network, comprising a conditional CNN and LSTM, integrates sequential images and global path data into a comprehensive state vector. Moreover, the incorporation of fuzzy logic in the study addresses problems arising from the independence of multiple motion commands. The CDQN has been demonstrated not only to be effective in creating directional plans but also in terms of learning efficiency and driving stability. Nevertheless, the model could benefit from additional features; it currently does not consider on-road obstacles. This gap in functionality suggests that future iterations of the model should focus on integrating obstacle avoidance mechanisms and accounting for traffic signals to enhance its utility and applicability in real-world driving scenarios.

Focusing on driving behavior prediction and motion planning, one study introduced a hierarchical IRL framework [9]. This design addresses driving behaviors across three distinct levels: driving patterns, discrete maneuvers, and continuous motion trajectories. Central to this approach is the incorporation of the actions of ego vehicles on future behaviors of surrounding entities. Integrating this predictive behavior into a chance-constrained partially observable Markov decision process (POMDP) leads to risk-bound motion plans. The accuracy demonstrated in predicting interactive driving behaviors and generating safe plans under complex conditions is evident. The challenges include refining predictions in scenarios with noisy observations and conducting comparative evaluations against other prediction and planning methodologies. Similarly, another study offers the CommonRoad-RL—a toolbox tailored to train and evaluate RL-based motion planners [10]. Its versatility lies in the configurable state spaces, action spaces, and rewards, allowing users to identify an ideal MDP tailored to their tasks. Among the key highlights are comparisons across varied reward definitions, vehicle models, and action paradigms. Moreover, it anticipates advancements such as MARL for cooperative driving, a range of integrated interfaces, and added support for an array of scenario specifications.

To improve learning an optimal policy that maximizes cumulative rewards, one study presented a model-free deep RL approach to continuous-state and continuous-action problems with episodic MDP [11]. By developing a modular DDPG framework to decompose the temporal automaton into correlated sub-tasks, the study showed improved performance in satisfying linear temporal logic specifications compared to standard DDPG. In another study, autonomous driving is approached as a hierarchical behavior and motion planning (HBMP) problem, aligning it with an RL problem where the reward is derived from the optimal cost of a lower-tier motion planner [12]. This alignment is facilitated by a sampling-based motion planner. The introduced sharable sensory data representation is implemented in the event-based simulator, simulation of urban mobility (SUMO) [13, 14], using imitation learning (IL). The effectiveness of the HBMP policy is demonstrated against counterparts on the CARLA platform, and its generalization capabilities are confirmed through real-world tests. Moreover, one study models traffic using a stochastic MDP, with both RL and IRL applied to achieve desired driving behaviors [15]. This approach offers tools to model traffic considering various parameters, such as lane numbers and the count of EVs. The inclusion of road geometry allows the driving policy to adjust based on road curvature. However, the model has limitations due to its simplified approach to vehicle velocities and point-mass representation. Future work aims to dynamically scale the MDP state in response to vehicle velocities.

A resource investigation into vehicle models reveals a range of simulation capabilities and the essential computational demands [16]. It serves as a guide through the strategic layers of decision-making and the diverse models of observation, encompassing both continuous and discrete states, as well as grid-based and camera-based solutions. Furthermore, it systematically arranges a variety of autonomous driving tasks, such as car-following, lane-keeping, trajectory tracking, smooth merging, and navigating dense traffic. In addition, one study examines the selection, growth, and refinement in pipeline methods, alongside exploring training and validation scenarios for end-to-end driving tasks [17]. With reviews of experimental platforms to inform strategy selection and a comparative analysis of pros and cons of each method, it equips individuals to make knowledgeable, system-level design decisions.

Motion planning for autonomous driving is a critical aspect of developing safe and efficient autonomous driving. This process involves generating a path that the vehicle will follow, taking into account various dynamic and static obstacles within the environment [18]. Despite significant advancements in this field, motion planning continues to present substantial challenges due to the complex nature of driving environments and the need for real-time responsiveness. One of the primary challenges in motion planning is ensuring safety and robustness in unpredictable traffic conditions. Autonomous vehicles must be capable of handling scenarios that involve pedestrians, cyclists, and other vehicles that may behave in unpredictable ways. Moreover, the motion planning system must be able to react instantaneously to sudden changes in the environment, such as a pedestrian stepping onto the road unexpectedly or another vehicle changing lanes abruptly. Another significant challenge is the computational complexity involved in motion planning. The system must process a vast amount of sensory data and perform complex calculations to determine the optimal path within fractions of a second. This requires not only powerful processing capabilities but also algorithms that can efficiently make decisions in high-dimensional spaces.

Incorporating machine learning, notably deep learning, into motion planning for autonomous driving is a significant area of development. This approach significantly augments the decision-making capabilities of autonomous driving. By learning from vast datasets encompassing diverse driving scenarios, deep learning models can improve the predictive accuracy of autonomous driving systems, enabling them to anticipate and adeptly navigate complex dynamic environments. Training these models to simulate experienced human driving behavior allows autonomous driving to execute sophisticated maneuvers and make split-second decisions that enhance both safety and efficiency on the road. This integration is key to evolving how autonomous systems adapt to the unpredictable variables of real-world driving. Another research direction is the development of more sophisticated algorithms for predictive modeling. These algorithms help autonomous driving anticipate future actions of other road users and adjust their own paths accordingly. Predictive models rely on historical data and real-time interactions, requiring continual updates and refinements to remain effective in diverse scenarios.

The exploration of hybrid systems in motion planning for autonomous driving is increasingly integrating both rule-based and learning-based methodologies. These systems merge the precision of rule-based algorithms, which ensure compliance with traffic laws and ethical guidelines, with the flexibility of learning-based approaches that adapt to the unpredictability of real-world environments. This synergy aims to enhance the accuracy and reliability of autonomous decision-making processes. Furthermore, there is a significant focus on advancing simulation technologies crucial for testing these motion planning algorithms. State-of-the-art simulation tools are indispensable for performing comprehensive evaluations within controlled virtual environments that closely replicate actual driving conditions. These technologies allow researchers to rigorously test a wide array of driving scenarios and edge cases, providing essential insights while mitigating the risks associated with physical road tests. Such advancements not only bolster the safety and efficacy of motion planning strategies but also expedite the development cycle of autonomous driving technologies. Incorporating advanced computational methods, sophisticated machine learning techniques, and robust simulation tools is pivotal in addressing the multifaceted challenges of motion planning for autonomous vehicles. The ongoing development and refinement of these tools are crucial for crafting efficient, safe, and reliable motion planning systems, which are fundamental to the future landscape of autonomous transportation. This iterative process of innovation and application underscores the dynamic field of autonomous vehicles, promising significant advancements in how these vehicles navigate and interact with their environments.

1.2 Deep learning-based trajectory prediction

Deep learning-based trajectory prediction (**Figure 2**) is essential for autonomous driving due to its critical role in anticipating future movements of nearby vehicles and pedestrians. This section explores the advancements in deep learning, specifically focusing on how techniques such as RNNs and LSTMs are leveraged to predict the trajectories of surrounding entities with high accuracy. These models process historical and real-time positional data to forecast the paths that these entities are likely to take, facilitating proactive and preventive maneuvering by autonomous vehicles. Such predictive capabilities are vital for enhancing safety, reducing collisions, and improving traffic flow. By harnessing these advancements, the future of autonomous driving promises safer, more efficient, and more responsive vehicles capable of navigating the complexities of real-world environments with a high degree of precision and foresight.

The field of trajectory prediction is pivotal for ensuring the safety and efficiency of autonomous driving. Recent research in this domain has been significantly influenced by deep learning techniques, which have brought substantial innovation and accuracy to these predictions. For example, one study introduces the trajectory prediction model, GRIP++, for autonomous driving vehicles [19]. This model demonstrates effectiveness in representing interactions among proximate objects via a graph and utilizes an encoder-decoder GRU-based architecture for predictions. GRIP++ has the capability to predict trajectories of all observed objects simultaneously,

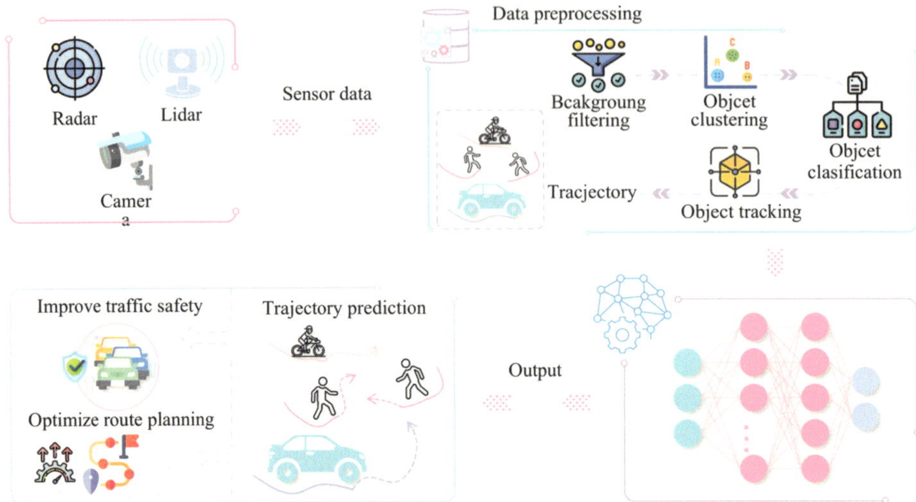

Figure 2.
Trajectory prediction in autonomous driving.

eliminating the limitations of models that predict singular traffic agents. Comparative analysis, leveraging highway and urban datasets, positions GRIP++ as superior, outpacing its peers in prediction accuracy and efficiency. An 83% improvement in urban scenarios over its predecessor, GRIP, underscores its efficacy. Further independent investigation can be carried out on the integration of GRIP++ with route planning and deep learning-based perception modules, ultimately testing this integration in prototype robotic cars. Another study introduces a graph-based spatial–temporal convolutional network (GSTCN) designed for predicting the paths of all vehicles in a scene [20]. It employs a weighted adjacency matrix to perceive and outline how nearby vehicles influence the one that is focused on. This feature allows GSTCN to capture the subtle spatial ties between vehicles. GSTCN has been demonstrated as an effective tool with its compact model size and fast inference speeds.

For heterogeneous multi-agent trajectory prediction, the researchers proposed a three-channel framework [21]. The representation of inter-agent interaction is accomplished using a directed edge-featured heterogeneous graph. This work introduces the heterogeneous edge-enhanced graph attention network for modeling this interaction and infuses a gate mechanism for selective map sharing across target agents. Validations, utilizing both urban and highway driving datasets, confirm the robust performance of the method. A standout feature is its proficiency in predicting multi-agent trajectories for an arbitrary cohort of heterogeneous agents.

LSTM networks are widely designed to capture and model temporal dependencies in sequential data, making them well-suited for predicting future trajectories based on past motion patterns. For example, delving into dynamic mixed traffic scenarios, one study includes LSTMs to predict longitudinal trajectories in a connected and autonomous vehicle environment [22]. It provides a comparative study of three LSTM models: Naïve LSTM, HS-LSTM, and attention-based LSTM. While the former mainly relies on historical trajectory data, the latter models incorporate nearby CAVs, emphasizing the importance of environmental awareness. Notably, the attention mechanism highlights the pivotal roles vehicles play in predicting trajectories, especially those in close proximity to the high-definition vehicles.

Progressing into highway trajectory analysis, an intention-aware LSTM network demonstrates an impressive ability to predict long-term vehicle trajectories with good precision [23]. This network excels due to its adaptability to different road geometries and its deep insight into the behaviors of surrounding vehicles, supporting advanced decision-making systems. Moreover, a shift toward vehicular interaction patterns is marked by the introduction of the structural LSTM, a learning model adept at handling multi-sequence data [24]. It not only tracks long-term trajectories but also emphasizes the significance of inter-vehicle dynamics. Its versatility in accommodating various road geometries and providing a comprehensive view of traffic interactions underscores its prowess in trajectory forecasting. In the complex environment of multi-lane intersections, an LSTM-RNN model is employed to predict irregular vehicle behaviors with accuracy [25]. Leveraging real-world data gathered by autonomous vehicles, this model stands out in its ability to anticipate complex maneuvers, particularly at intersections where turns are involved. Its performance, when compared to baseline models such as those assuming constant velocity, showcases improved efficiency and potential for real-world application. These deep learning models, especially RNNs and LSTMs, have proven their merit in enhancing trajectory prediction capabilities for autonomous vehicles. Their grasp of vehicle interactions, flexibility in various traffic conditions, and emphasis on understanding intent and environmental context make a strong argument for their ongoing relevance in the advancement of autonomous navigation.

NeuroTrajectory, an integration of neuroevolution and local state trajectory learning, enhances the robustness of trajectory prediction [26]. This approach leverages occupancy grid sequences and employs multi-objective Pareto optimization to embed learned trajectories directly into the weights of a dedicated DNN. The model effectively merges real and synthetic data, with the latter generated from the GridSim simulator [27], showcasing proficiency in its function. Notably, NeuroTrajectory outperforms the dynamic window approach baseline in local trajectory prediction for autonomous vehicles, indicating its practical application potential. In the context of urban environments, CoverNet emerges as an effective method that redefines trajectory prediction as a classification task across a wide array of possible trajectories [28]. The distinction of CoverNet lies in its ability to ensure extensive state space coverage, eliminate dynamically infeasible trajectories, and prevent mode collapse. The dynamic generation of trajectory sets based on the present state of the agent further enhances its performance. This technique has proven its effectiveness by outperforming existing methods in real-world dataset comparisons.

By leveraging multi-modal trajectory predictions, one study designed memory-augmented networks for multiple trajectories (MANTRA) [29]. With associative memory, MANTRA understands the complexities of future trajectory predictions. It offers tools to predict varied trajectories and learn new patterns, thus continually improving itself. Using RNNs, it delves deep into past and future trajectory embeddings, with external memory aiding in effective storage and retrieval. Additionally, by incorporating semantic scene maps through a CNN, it integrates scene knowledge into the decoding process. Each model, from neuroevolutionary strategies to memory-augmented frameworks, contributes to trajectory prediction for safer, smarter autonomous driving.

Trajectory prediction for autonomous driving is essential for ensuring the safe and efficient operation of vehicles in complex and dynamic environments. This aspect of autonomous vehicle technology involves forecasting the future positions of nearby pedestrians, vehicles, and other elements within the driving environment, based on current and historical sensor data. Despite significant advancements in this area, trajectory prediction remains fraught with challenges, largely due to the unpredictable nature of real-world interactions and the high degree of accuracy required for safe navigation. One major challenge in trajectory prediction is the inherent uncertainty in human behavior. Pedestrians, cyclists, and other drivers may act unpredictably, making it difficult to accurately forecast their future movements. Compounding this issue is the variability in environmental conditions—such as weather changes, variable lighting, and road conditions—that can further influence behaviors and trajectory paths. The high dimensionality of the data involved in making these predictions also poses a significant computational challenge. Autonomous vehicles must process data from multiple sensors, including cameras, radar, and lidar, in real time. This processing must not only be accurate but also incredibly fast, as delays in data processing can lead to outdated information, potentially compromising the ability to make safe decisions.

Research in trajectory prediction is actively exploring several promising avenues to overcome these challenges. Deep learning models, particularly those involving RNNs and LSTMs, are at the forefront, due to their ability to effectively process and make predictions based on sequential data. These models can learn complex patterns in movement and are increasingly being trained on large datasets that include a diverse range of driving scenarios and behaviors. Another significant area of research is the development of probabilistic models that can handle uncertainty more effectively. These models are designed to provide not just a single predicted trajectory but a range of possible future trajectories, each with associated probabilities. This probabilistic approach allows autonomous systems to plan paths that are robust to potential deviations in predicted trajectories. Moreover, the integration of multi-agent systems into trajectory prediction algorithms is gaining attention. This approach considers the interactive behaviors of multiple agents within the environment, providing a more holistic view of potential future movements. By understanding how agents influence the trajectories of one another, these models can make more informed predictions.

Enhancing trajectory prediction models by integrating contextual and semantic information is becoming increasingly significant in the development of autonomous driving systems. By recognizing and analyzing the context of different driving environments—whether it is a bustling city intersection or a quiet suburban area—models can tailor their predictions to reflect typical behaviors expected in these varying settings. This approach helps in achieving more precise and reliable trajectory predictions. Trajectory prediction in autonomous driving encapsulates a complex interplay of advanced machine learning techniques, real-time data processing, and a nuanced understanding of human behavior and environmental variables. The challenges in this field are substantial, as the technology must accurately anticipate the movement of multiple, unpredictable agents in diverse conditions. Despite these difficulties, continuous innovations in technology and methodological approaches are progressively expanding the capabilities of autonomous vehicles, driving forward improvements in their safety, reliability, and operational efficiency.

1.3 End-to-end learning for autonomous control

End-to-end learning for autonomous control is vital for autonomous driving due to its integral role in directly translating sensor inputs into vehicular control commands. This section reviews the development of deep learning in the context of end-to-end learning, showcasing how neural networks, particularly CNNs and DRL among others, enable a vehicle to perform complex driving tasks autonomously by processing raw data from cameras and other sensors directly into steering, acceleration, and braking decisions (**Figure 3**). This streamlined approach eliminates the traditional segmentation of tasks such as detection, recognition, and decision-making, potentially leading to more natural driving behaviors and reduced processing time.

In the realm of autonomous control, end-to-end learning emerges as a dynamic frontier. Several key studies provide insights into distinct approaches, each demonstrating the adaptability and sophistication intrinsic to end-to-end learning in navigating autonomous systems. For example, one study emphasizes the value of simulation for training autonomous systems, particularly in replicating challenging real-world scenarios [30]. They designed VISTA: Virtual Image Synthesis and Transformation for Autonomy, a simulator that stands apart by offering end-to-end data-driven training for autonomous vehicles. VISTA excels in its ability to train agents within a broad spectrum of feasible trajectories, all synthesized from data anchored on a single trajectory by a human driver. In a subsequent study, the authors presented VISTA 2.0, which integrates multiple sensor modalities, including RGB cameras, 3D LiDAR, and event-based cameras, enabling diverse and realistic simulations [31]. By leveraging real-world datasets, VISTA 2.0 enriches the data available for policy learning, facilitating sim-to-real transfer without modification. Deployed on a full-scale autonomous vehicle, VISTA 2.0 demonstrates robustness and efficacy in training perception-to-control policies across various sensor types.

A paradigm shift toward integrating spatial–temporal feature learning in autonomous driving is marked by ST-P3, which transitions from traditional multi-stage discrete pipelines to an end-to-end methodology [32]. This approach advocates for the fusion of perception, prediction, and planning tasks, introducing techniques such as egocentric-aligned accumulation, dual pathway modeling, and temporal-based refinement. Together, these innovations present a comprehensive vision-based system for autonomous driving, notable for its creativity and interpretability. Following this, SuperDriver AI emerges as a forward-thinking, end-to-end, learning-based

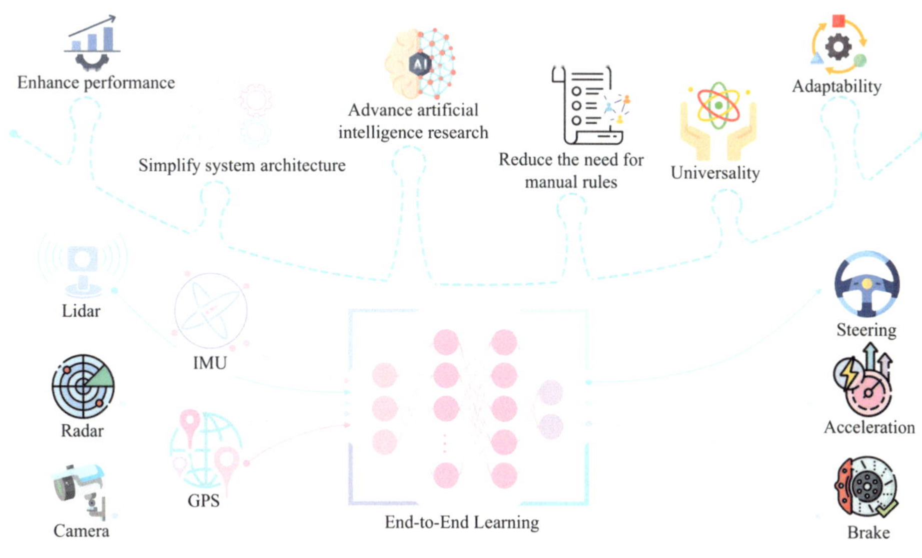

Figure 3.
End-to-end control in autonomous driving.

autonomous driving system utilizing DNNs [33]. It advances beyond simple maneuver determination by incorporating a visual attention module, thereby significantly enhancing the robustness and interpretability of the system.

A lane-keeping strategy that integrates end-to-end learning with a multi-state model was introduced, centered around a 3D CNN-LSTM end-to-end model with three tailored parameter sets for different driving maneuvers [34]. This multi-state approach demonstrates effective lane-keeping accuracy in the TORCS simulator, surpassing traditional single-model systems. Additionally, a specialized combination of CNN and LSTM was proposed, designed to extract both temporal and spatial features [35]. This research highlights the capability to predict steering wheel angles by analyzing temporal changes, showcasing the effectiveness of combining these technologies.

Incorporating end-to-end learning with both DDPG and IL, one study introduced dual experience pools for end-to-end learning of driving strategies [36]. Initial data from IL accelerates the DDPG learning speed. The subsequent self-learning of the algorithm further refines its proficiency. Trials on the TORCS simulator elucidated the superior convergence and performance of this DDPG-IL algorithm over its conventional DDPG counterpart. A notable improvement opportunity lies in the current random data retrieval method, which can potentially be optimized in future research. For heightened clarity and precision, the meticulous manual classification of image features is emphasized in the end-to-end autonomous vehicle controller as demonstrated in [37]. It also investigates different driving conditions and the varying significance of specific road segments. Recognizing the potential of automation, future endeavors should include utilizing techniques such as fully CNN for automatic feature classification. Furthermore, another study positions an end-to-end model as the foundation for holistic autonomous driving software stacks [38]. The integration of deep learning techniques for both lateral and longitudinal control is pivotal. By employing the TORCS simulator, the research establishes the potential of neural networks to predict vehicle speed and steering, offering an AI-driven approach as opposed to deterministic rules.

As driving environments become denser and more dynamic, the limitations of conventional sensor fusion methods are increasingly apparent. These weaknesses become evident in situations that require global contextual reasoning, such as navigating multi-directional traffic at uncontrolled intersections. To solve this issue, TransFuser, a revolutionary approach designed to address the challenges mentioned above, was introduced [39]. As a multi-modal fusion transformer, TransFuser presents an effective methodology for combining image and LiDAR data. At its core lies the attention mechanism, which allows the model to dynamically focus on and prioritize key segments of the input data. The standout feature of TransFuser is its ability to understand global contexts, giving the vehicle a comprehensive view of its environment. By breaking free from the limitations of purely geometry-based approaches and leveraging the power of attention, TransFuser offers an enhanced understanding of urban terrains.

End-to-end learning for autonomous control represents a streamlined approach in the field of autonomous systems, where control decisions are derived directly from sensory inputs using deep learning models. This approach simplifies the traditional multi-stage pipeline of perception, decision-making, and control into a single model that processes inputs and outputs control commands, aiming for more cohesive and efficient decision-making processes. Despite its promise, end-to-end learning presents numerous challenges and opens up various avenues for research. A primary challenge in end-to-end learning is the sheer complexity of modeling the entire control logic of an autonomous system in one go. The model must handle high-dimensional sensory data, such as images and LiDAR readings, and translate these directly into actuation commands. This requires the neural network to not only understand the environment but also to make intricate driving decisions, which involves a high level of abstraction and generalization from raw data.

End-to-end learning systems in autonomous control heavily depend on extensive and diverse training datasets. These systems are trained to handle a broad spectrum of scenarios and conditions to ensure effective performance. However, the acquisition and labeling of such comprehensive datasets can be incredibly labor-intensive and financially demanding. Moreover, maintaining the ability to generalize effectively to new, unobserved scenarios—critical for real-world application—poses additional challenges. Ensuring robustness against overfitting, where models perform well on training data but poorly on unseen data, is crucial for the practical deployment of these systems in dynamic environments. Another concern is the interpretability and safety of end-to-end learning models. Since decision-making is inherently opaque in DNNs, understanding and validating the decisions made by such systems can be challenging. This is particularly critical in safety-sensitive applications such as autonomous driving, where understanding the rationale behind decisions is crucial for trust and regulatory approval.

From a research standpoint, advancing the architecture and training methodologies to enhance the robustness and efficiency of end-to-end models presents a substantial opportunity. Employing techniques like transfer learning—which allows the application of insights gained from one task to improve performance in another—and domain adaptation—which optimizes model efficacy across varying environments—stands out as particularly promising. Improving the interpretability of these systems also marks a critical area of research. Techniques such as feature visualization and attention mechanisms can clarify the decision-making processes within models, making them more comprehensible to developers, regulators, and users alike. Such transparency is crucial not only for fine-tuning and advancing these models but also for fostering trust and encouraging wider adoption. Furthermore, ensuring that end-to-end systems can operate in real time is essential. Research focused on optimizing neural networks to enhance processing speed without losing accuracy is vital. This might involve model compression techniques or the implementation of specialized hardware accelerations, which could significantly bolster their practical application. While end-to-end learning for autonomous control heralds a significant shift in the design of autonomous systems, it also requires surmounting notable technical challenges. Addressing these through cutting-edge research can open up new possibilities in autonomous technology, enhancing adaptability, efficiency, and safety in complex, real-world settings.

1.4 Safe and explainable control with deep learning

Ensuring safe and comprehensible control mechanisms through deep learning is essential in autonomous driving, as it supports the capability to execute decisions that are both informed and transparent, which are crucial for ensuring vehicle safety. This section investigates the progress in deep learning focused on boosting both safety and clarity in the control systems of autonomous driving (**Figure 4**). It emphasizes the use of advanced techniques such as layer-wise relevance propagation (LRP) and shapley additive explanations (SHAP) within the operational frameworks of neural networks.

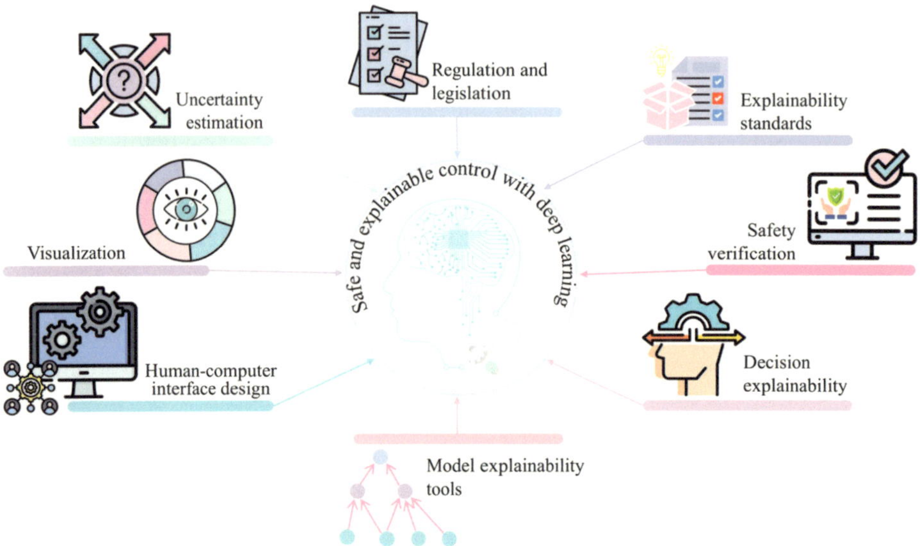

Figure 4.
Safe and explainable control in autonomous driving.

Moreover, the use of feature visualization and activation mapping enables engineers to identify specific features that activate certain layers of a neural network, crucial for ensuring the focus aligns with safety-critical standards. These techniques not only adhere to stringent safety protocols but also empower engineers and end-users to verify and trust the artificial intelligence guiding the system. By improving transparency and safety in autonomous vehicle control systems, deep learning is paving the way for these vehicles' practical deployment in complex, real-world settings. These technological advancements are vital for reinforcing the safety protocols of autonomous vehicles and fostering broader acceptance and trust in AI-driven systems.

In recent years, there has been a notable increase in interest surrounding XAI [40–42]. Various approaches perceive XAI based on their specific needs and perspectives. For example, one study highlights how different elements of autonomous driving can be elucidated and made transparent through XAI [43]. The review also discusses current solutions that bring clarity and interpretability to these aspects of autonomous vehicles. While urban mobility research and initiatives largely focus on vehicular issues such as congestion and pollution, the safety of pedestrians—a vulnerable segment—is often overlooked. By merging public data, expansive street imagery, and advanced computer vision techniques, one study crafts a methodology for enhancing both vehicular and pedestrian safety [44]. This methodology, aided by specialized neural networks, produces a comprehensive hazard map for urban terrains, identifying zones needing safety interventions. Such a structure is suggested as an auxiliary resource for urban planners and policymakers.

XAI in autonomous driving has led to the development of several innovative frameworks. For example, through a case study analyzing a post-accident scenario, the designed framework reveals its ability to create smarter driving systems [45]. It provides a pathway for better debugging, refining, and enhancing the intelligence behind intelligent driving. Future hands-on work aims to integrate visual question answering with DRL for clear, understandable visual action interpretation. With the rapid advancements in the autonomous driving sector, ensuring vehicular safety becomes paramount. This investigation leverages sensor data from self-driving vehicles to devise a comprehensive risk assessment catering to various potential collision scenarios. Supported by machine learning models, another study introduced a method for deducing vehicular risk [46]. The resulting models not only demonstrate high performance but also show adaptability across diverse datasets. Furthermore, the accompanying explanation methods empower developers by highlighting crucial attributes for risk reduction and aiding in model debugging, especially in safety-critical situations.

In an effort to comprehend the dynamics between interactive systems, one study focuses on grounded relational inference (GRI) to infer the semantic relationships between agents [47]. It incorporates structured reward functions to ensure that the relational latent space reflects behaviors that are meaningful and supported by expert knowledge. This approach elucidates the dynamic behavior of vehicles through semantic interaction graphs, thereby enhancing the transparency of vehicular actions. Similarly, another study delves into understanding and explaining DNNs, shedding light on their ability to predict random data [48]. Given the unpredictable environments that autonomous systems navigate, the study investigates the decision-making processes of the DNNs. Furthermore, by employing RL with a safety supervisor, another study underscores the importance of human-centric models, particularly in lane-changing decisions [49]. Through the piloting and validation of a human lane-changing model, RL can develop a driving policy that prioritizes safety and stability. The results demonstrate a significant reduction in collisions during both the training and implementation phases, without compromising training performance."

Cooperative computing is enhancing the capabilities of autonomous vehicles, promising improved performance and safety through a diverse range of data sources. However, efficiently and securely managing data from various sources remains a complex challenge. To address this challenge, one study introduces federated learning, which offers a decentralized learning approach aiming to ensure secure data sharing between vehicles [50]. With privacy and cooperation at the forefront, this study combines Transformers, federated learning, and cooperative perception. It proposes a hierarchical structure for Transformers in vehicles, suggesting an organizational framework that unites vehicular Transformers, federated vehicular Transformers, and the federation of vehicular Transformers, all collaborating with a focus on privacy.

One review and categorization of classical software safety methods in the context of machine learning algorithms provides a holistic picture [51]. Recognizing the need to combine engineering safety strategies with advanced machine learning techniques, this research highlights the multidisciplinary effort required to ensure the safety of autonomous vehicles. Encompassing domains such as human-computer interactions, machine learning, and software and hardware engineering, the study underscores potential avenues of research and collaboration to enhance the dependability and safety of data-driven systems.

The integration of safe and explainable control mechanisms using deep learning into autonomous driving systems is a critical focus area, addressing two of the most pressing challenges in the field: ensuring the safety of autonomous actions and enhancing the transparency of decision-making processes. While deep learning offers sophisticated capabilities in handling complex driving scenarios, its application in safety-critical systems such as autonomous vehicles necessitates a highly cautious approach and a clear understanding of the decision-making process. One of the paramount challenges in implementing deep learning for autonomous driving is ensuring that these systems adhere to stringent safety standards. Autonomous vehicles must make decisions that minimize risk not only to the vehicle and its passengers but also to other road users, including pedestrians and cyclists. This requires an exceptionally high level of reliability in perception and decision-making systems to correctly interpret sensory data and act safely under various driving conditions. Techniques such as redundancy, where multiple systems check and balance each other, and rigorous scenario testing are commonly employed to enhance safety. Furthermore, recent advances in predictive safety models use deep learning to forecast potential hazards and adjust vehicle behavior preemptively, thereby reducing the risk of accidents.

Alongside safety, the explainability of autonomous systems is crucial for gaining public trust and regulatory approval. Deep learning models, often criticized for their "black-box" nature, are inherently difficult to interpret, making it challenging to trace how decisions are made. Enhancing the explainability of these systems involves developing methods that can elucidate the reasoning behind the outputs. Techniques such as LRP and visualization of activation maps help in identifying what the model is focusing on when making decisions. Moreover, incorporating rule-based systems alongside deep learning can offer a balance between high performance and decision traceability, providing clear rationales for actions taken by the vehicle.

Emerging research is increasingly focusing on hybrid models that combine the robust capabilities of deep learning with the safety and interpretability of more traditional control systems. These hybrid approaches aim to leverage the strengths of both paradigms—utilizing deep learning for complex perception and decision-making tasks, while rule-based components ensure compliance with predefined safety and operational guidelines. Another promising area is the development of robust simulation tools that allow for extensive testing of deep learning-based control systems in a wide array of driving scenarios, including rare and dangerous situations not frequently encountered on the road. These simulations help in fine-tuning the systems for safety and reliability without the risks associated with physical testing. Lastly, there is an increasing interest in the development of frameworks for continuous learning and adaptation in the field. These frameworks would allow vehicles to learn from new data collected during operation, adjusting and improving their decision-making algorithms over time while maintaining high levels of safety and explainability. In conclusion, while the challenges of integrating safe and explainable control with deep learning in autonomous driving are significant, ongoing technological advancements and research efforts are opening new pathways for development. These efforts are essential for building autonomous driving systems that are not only highly efficient and capable but also trustworthy and user-friendly, paving the way for broader acceptance and deployment.

2. Conclusion

The integration of deep learning into the planning and control mechanisms of autonomous vehicles has ushered in a new era of innovation and capability. Throughout this section, we briefly explore how advanced algorithms—ranging from reinforcement learning techniques to both supervised and self-supervised learning models—address the complex challenges inherent in autonomous navigation. These technologies enable vehicles to learn optimal action sequences, predict the trajectories of surrounding objects with increasing accuracy, and make real-time decisions that prioritize safety, efficiency, and passenger comfort. The adoption of end-to-end learning approaches further streamlines the decision-making pipeline by directly mapping sensor inputs to control actions. While these methods hold significant promise for reducing system latency and complexity, they also introduce challenges related to interpretability and safety assurances. The incorporation of XAI techniques is a critical step toward mitigating these concerns, providing transparency in the decision-making processes, and fostering greater trust among users and regulators. While the progress in deep learning applications is substantial, key areas warrant further investigation. Challenges such as crafting effective reward structures in reinforcement learning, developing robust methods for uncertainty management in trajectory forecasting, and reinforcing the transparency and reliability of end-to-end systems require ongoing exploration. Successfully addressing these issues will be critical to advancing the dependability and societal acceptance of autonomous vehicles.

Acknowledgements

The author acknowledges the usage of Grammarly for language polishing of the manuscript.

Author details

Jingyuan Zhao* and Andrew F. Burke
Institute of Transportation Studies, University of California Davis, CA, USA

*Address all correspondence to: jyzhao@ucdavis.edu

References

[1] Van Brummelen J, O'Brien M, Gruyer D, Najjaran H. Autonomous vehicle perception: The technology of today and tomorrow. Transportation Research Part C: Emerging Technologies. 2018;**89**:384-406

[2] Zhao J, Zhao W, Deng B, Wang Z, Zhang F, Zheng W, et al. Autonomous driving system: A comprehensive survey. Expert Systems with Applications. 2023;**242**:122836

[3] Kuutti S, Bowden R, Jin Y, Barber P, Fallah S. A survey of deep learning applications to autonomous vehicle control. IEEE Transactions on Intelligent Transportation Systems. 2020;**22**(2):712-733

[4] Schwarting W, Alonso-Mora J, Rus D. Planning and decision-making for autonomous vehicles. Annual Review of Control, Robotics, and Autonomous Systems. 2018;**1**(1):187-210

[5] Kiran BR, Sobh I, Talpaert V, Mannion P, Al Sallab AA, Yogamani S, et al. Deep reinforcement learning for autonomous driving: A survey. IEEE Transactions on Intelligent Transportation Systems. 2021;**23**(6):4909-4926

[6] Huang Y, Du J, Yang Z, Zhou Z, Zhang L, Chen H. A survey on trajectory-prediction methods for autonomous driving. IEEE Transactions on Intelligent Vehicles. 2022;**7**(3):652-674

[7] Chen L, Wu P, Chitta K, Jaeger B, Geiger A, Li H. End-to-end autonomous driving: Challenges and frontiers. IEEE Transactions on Pattern Analysis and Machine Intelligence. 2024;**46**:10164-10183

[8] Chen L, Hu X, Tang B, Cheng Y. Conditional DQN-based motion planning with fuzzy logic for autonomous driving. IEEE Transactions on Intelligent Transportation Systems. 2020;**23**(4):2966-2977

[9] Li D, Wu Y, Bai B, Hao Q. Behavior and interaction-aware motion planning for autonomous driving vehicles based on hierarchical intention and motion prediction. In: 2020 IEEE 23rd International Conference on Intelligent Transportation Systems (ITSC). Piscataway, NJ, USA: IEEE; 2020. pp. 1-8

[10] Wang X, Krasowski H, Althoff M. CommonRoad-RL: A configurable reinforcement learning environment for motion planning of autonomous vehicles. In: 2021 IEEE International Intelligent Transportation Systems Conference (ITSC). Piscataway, NJ, USA: IEEE; 2021. pp. 466-472

[11] Cai M, Hasanbeig M, Xiao S, Abate A, Kan Z. Modular deep reinforcement learning for continuous motion planning with temporal logic. IEEE Robotics and Automation Letters. 2021;**6**(4):7973-7980

[12] Wang J, Wang Y, Zhang D, Yang Y, Xiong R. Learning hierarchical behavior and motion planning for autonomous driving. In: 2020 IEEE/RSJ International Conference on Intelligent Robots and Systems (IROS). Piscataway, NJ, USA: IEEE; 2020. pp. 2235-2242

[13] Krajzewicz D. Traffic simulation with SUMO–simulation of urban mobility. In: Fundamentals of Traffic Simulation. New York, NY: Springer; 2010. pp. 269-293

[14] Krajzewicz D, Erdmann J, Behrisch M, Bieker L. Recent development and applications of

SUMO-simulation of urban Mobility. International Journal on Advances in Systems and Measurements. 2012;**5**(3&4):128-138

[15] You C, Lu J, Filev D, Tsiotras P. Advanced planning for autonomous vehicles using reinforcement learning and deep inverse reinforcement learning. Robotics and Autonomous Systems. 2019;**114**:1-18

[16] Aradi S. Survey of deep reinforcement learning for motion planning of autonomous vehicles. IEEE Transactions on Intelligent Transportation Systems. 2020;**23**(2):740-759

[17] Teng S, Hu X, Deng P, Li B, Li Y, Ai Y, et al. Motion planning for autonomous driving: The state of the art and future perspectives. IEEE Transactions on Intelligent Vehicles. 2023;**8**:3692-3711

[18] Nan J, Ge Z, Ye X, Burke AF, Zhao J. Model predictive control for autonomous vehicle path tracking through optimized kinematics. Results in Engineering. 2024;**24**:103123

[19] Li X, Ying X, Chuah MC. Grip++: Enhanced graph-based interaction-aware trajectory prediction for autonomous driving. arXiv. 2019. Available from: https://arxiv.org/abs/1907.07792

[20] Sheng Z, Xu Y, Xue S, Li D. Graph-based spatial-temporal convolutional network for vehicle trajectory prediction in autonomous driving. IEEE Transactions on Intelligent Transportation Systems. 2022;**23**(10):17654-17665

[21] Mo X, Huang Z, Xing Y, Lv C. Multi-agent trajectory prediction with heterogeneous edge-enhanced graph attention network. IEEE Transactions on Intelligent Transportation Systems. 2022;**23**(7):9554-9567

[22] Lin L, Gong S, Peeta S, Wu X. Long short-term memory-based human-driven vehicle longitudinal trajectory prediction in a connected and autonomous vehicle environment. Transportation Research Record. 2021;**2675**(6):380-390

[23] Xin L, Wang P, Chan CY, Chen J, Li SE, Cheng B. Intention-aware long horizon trajectory prediction of surrounding vehicles using dual LSTM networks. In: 2018 21st International Conference on Intelligent Transportation Systems (ITSC). Piscataway, NJ, USA: IEEE; 2018. pp. 1441-1446

[24] Hou L, Xin L, Li SE, Cheng B, Wang W. Interactive trajectory prediction of surrounding road users for autonomous driving using structural-LSTM network. IEEE Transactions on Intelligent Transportation Systems. 2019;**21**(11):4615-4625

[25] Jeong Y, Kim S, Yi K. Surround vehicle motion prediction using LSTM-RNN for motion planning of autonomous vehicles at multi-lane turn intersections. IEEE Open Journal of Intelligent Transportation Systems. 2020;**1**:2-14

[26] Grigorescu SM, Trasnea B, Marina L, Vasilcoi A, Cocias T. Neurotrajectory: A neuroevolutionary approach to local state trajectory learning for autonomous vehicles. IEEE Robotics and Automation Letters. 2019;**4**(4):3441-3448

[27] Buyya R, Murshed M. Gridsim: A toolkit for the modeling and simulation of distributed resource management and scheduling for grid computing. Concurrency and Computation: Practice and Experience. 2002;**14**(13-15):1175-1220

[28] Phan-Minh T, Grigore EC, Boulton FA, Beijbom O, Wolff EM.

Covernet: Multimodal behavior prediction using trajectory sets. In: Proceedings of the IEEE/CVF Conference on Computer Vision and Pattern Recognition. Piscataway, NJ, USA: EEE; 2020. pp. 14074-14083

[29] Marchetti F, Becattini F, Seidenari L, Bimbo AD. Mantra: Memory augmented networks for multiple trajectory prediction. In: Proceedings of the IEEE/CVF Conference on Computer Vision and Pattern Recognition. 2020. pp. 7143-7152

[30] Amini A, Gilitschenski I, Phillips J, Moseyko J, Banerjee R, Karaman S, et al. Learning robust control policies for end-to-end autonomous driving from data-driven simulation. IEEE Robotics and Automation Letters. 2020;**5**(2):1143-1150

[31] Amini A, Wang TH, Gilitschenski I, Schwarting W, Liu Z, Han S, et al. Vista 2.0: An open, data-driven simulator for multimodal sensing and policy learning for autonomous vehicles. In: 2022 International Conference on Robotics and Automation (ICRA). Piscataway, NJ, USA: IEEE; 2022. pp. 2419-2426

[32] Hu S, Chen L, Wu P, Li H, Yan J, Tao D. St-p3: End-to-end vision-based autonomous driving via spatial-temporal feature learning. In: European Conference on Computer Vision. Cham: Springer Nature Switzerland; 2022. pp. 533-549

[33] Aoki S, Yamamoto I, Shiotsuka D, Inoue Y, Tokuhiro K, Miwa K. SuperDriverAI: Towards design and implementation for end-to-end learning-based autonomous driving. In: 2023 IEEE Vehicular Networking Conference (VNC). Piscataway, NJ, USA: IEEE; 2023. pp. 195-198

[34] Yuan W, Yang M, Li H, Wang C, Wang B. End-to-end learning for high-precision lane keeping via multi-state model. CAAI Transactions on Intelligence Technology. 2018;**3**(4):185-190

[35] Lee MJ, Ha YG. Autonomous driving control using end-to-end deep learning. In: 2020 IEEE International Conference on Big Data and Smart Computing (BigComp). Piscataway, NJ, USA: IEEE; 2020. pp. 470-473

[36] Zou Q, Xiong K, Hou Y. An end-to-end learning of driving strategies based on DDPG and imitation learning. In: 2020 Chinese Control and Decision Conference (CCDC). Piscataway, NJ, USA: IEEE; 2020. pp. 3190-3195

[37] Yang S, Wang W, Liu C, Deng W, Hedrick JK. Feature analysis and selection for training an end-to-end autonomous vehicle controller using deep learning approach. In: 2017 IEEE Intelligent Vehicles Symposium (IV). Piscataway, NJ, USA: IEEE; 2017. pp. 1033-1038

[38] Sharma S, Tewolde G, Kwon J. Lateral and longitudinal motion control of autonomous vehicles using deep learning. In: 2019 IEEE International Conference on Electro Information Technology (EIT). Piscataway, NJ, USA: IEEE; 2019. pp. 1-5

[39] Chitta K, Prakash A, Jaeger B, Yu Z, Renz K, Geiger A. Transfuser: Imitation with transformer-based sensor fusion for autonomous driving. IEEE Transactions on Pattern Analysis and Machine Intelligence. 2022;**45**:12878-12895

[40] Das A, Rad P. Opportunities and challenges in explainable artificial intelligence (xai): A survey. arXiv. 2020. DOI: 10.48550/arXiv.2006.11371

[41] Došilović FK, Brčić M, Hlupić N. Explainable artificial intelligence: A

survey. In: 2018 41st International Convention on Information and Communication Technology, Electronics and Microelectronics (MIPRO). Piscataway, NJ, USA: IEEE; 2018. pp. 210-215

[42] Angelov PP, Soares EA, Jiang R, Arnold NI, Atkinson PM. Explainable artificial intelligence: An analytical review. Wiley Interdisciplinary Reviews: Data Mining and Knowledge Discovery. 2021;**11**(5):e1424

[43] Hussain F, Hussain R, Hossain E. Explainable artificial intelligence (XAI): An engineering perspective. arXiv. 2021. DOI: 10.48550/arXiv.2101.03613

[44] Bustos C, Rhoads D, Solé-Ribalta A, Masip D, Arenas A, Lapedriza A, et al. Explainable, automated urban interventions to improve pedestrian and vehicle safety. Transportation Research Part C: Emerging Technologies. 2021;**125**:103018

[45] Atakishiyev S, Salameh M, Yao H, Goebel R. Towards safe, explainable, and regulated autonomous driving. In Explainable Artificial Intelligence for Intelligent Transportation Systems. CRC Press; 2021. pp. 32-52

[46] Nahata R, Omeiza D, Howard R, Kunze L. Assessing and explaining collision risk in dynamic environments for autonomous driving safety. In: 2021 IEEE International Intelligent Transportation Systems Conference (ITSC). Piscataway, NJ, USA: IEEE; 2021. pp. 223-230

[47] Dassanayake PM, Anjum A, Bashir AK, Bacon J, Saleem R, Manning W. A deep learning based explainable control system for reconfigurable networks of edge devices. IEEE Transactions on Network Science and Engineering. 2021;**9**(1):7-19

[48] Tang C, Srishankar N, Martin S, Tomizuka M. Grounded relational inference: Domain knowledge driven explainable autonomous driving. IEEE Transactions on Intelligent Transportation Systems. 2021;**25**(9):10617-10635

[49] Chen D, Jiang L, Wang Y, Li Z. Autonomous driving using safe reinforcement learning by incorporating a regret-based human lane-changing decision model. In: 2020 American Control Conference (ACC). Piscataway, NJ, USA: IEEE; 2020. pp. 4355-4361

[50] Tian Y, Wang J, Wang Y, Zhao C, Yao F, Wang X. Federated vehicular transformers and their federations: Privacy-preserving computing and cooperation for autonomous driving. IEEE Transactions on Intelligent Vehicles. 2022;7(3):456-465

[51] Mohseni S, Pitale M, Singh V, Wang Z. Practical solutions for machine learning safety in autonomous vehicles. arXiv. DOI: 10.48550/arXiv.1912.09630

Chapter 6

Virtual Verification and Validation of Autonomous Vehicles: Toolchain and Workflow

Alexandru Forrai, Mohsen Alirezaei, Tajinder Singh, Amit Gali and Jeroen Ploeg

Abstract

The complexity and efficient development of Autonomous Vehicles (AVs) require robust testing and validation methods to ensure their safety and reliability. This book chapter presents Siemens' autonomy toolchain for testing and virtual validation of Advanced Driver Assistance Systems (ADAS) and AV functions. The approach integrates scenario-based testing, virtual validation, and compliance with the applicable regulations and standards, such as the International Organization for Standardization (ISO). Relying on the multi-pillar safety validation framework proposed by United Nations Economic Commission for Europe (UN-ECE), and EU regulations, Siemens' toolchain enables efficient scenario extraction, critical scenario creation, and large-scale virtual validation. By addressing both software infrastructure and scenario generation, Siemens contributes to enhancing the reliability and safety of ADAS and AV systems.

Keywords: autonomous vehicles, virtual verification and validation, scenario-based testing, workflow, toolchain

1. Introduction

The market of Advanced Driver Assistance Systems (ADAS) and Autonomous Vehicles (AVs) is growing, driven by advancement in sensor technologies, artificial intelligence and the need of safer and efficient transportation. This section introduces the market of ADAS and AV, main challenges associated with AV development, scenario-based testing and overview of the proposed approach.

1.1 ADAS and AV market and main challenges

Incremental development and acceptance of automated driving technology currently lead to rapid adaptation of ADAS and AV technology. These systems provide enhanced safety features and a higher level of automation. The ADAS features of lane-keep assist, adaptive cruise control, emergency braking, and traffic sign recognition have contributed to achieving the different levels of vehicle automation. Finally, with the AV technology, the vehicle takes control of driving tasks, reducing the driver to a passenger to some extent.

Many vehicle manufacturers and suppliers have invested resources in developing AV technology as there is a market demand, particularly with shared mobility services, public transport, and logistics. Many research findings have predicted that the market for ADAS and AV will keep growing in the upcoming years.

One of the market research reports shows that the market will grow by 11.9% [1]. Another research by Mckinsey and Company provides the market prediction for the upcoming years, shown in **Figure 1** [2]. This research emphasizes growth in the ADAS and AV market up to 300 billion dollars by 2035 with level 4 automation responsible for the largest market share.

Furthermore, over the past few years, advancements in networks and technology have enhanced communication between the vehicles and infrastructure. Connected, Cooperative, and Automated Mobility (CCAM) has broadened the autonomous driving capabilities by providing transport facilities to people who cannot drive, delivering goods when human mobility is restricted, and in remote areas [3].

CCAM also has the capability to improve urban transportation efficiency by minimizing accidents and reducing CO_2 emissions. In a holistic view, CCAM relies on intelligent infrastructure that includes smart roadside units (RSUs) and Vehicle-to-Everything (V2X) communication. High speed and real-time communication is necessary between the vehicles and their surroundings and also traffic telematics - which collects, processes, and utilizes the traffic data and provides it to the relevant autonomous vehicles.

These features will provide vital information such as traffic jam warnings, accident warnings, better alternate routes, taxi information, parking lot information, etc. On the other hand, the advanced technology of AVs faces different challenges, among which some of the major challenges are:

1. *Scalability and interoperability* – To scale the AV operations across different regions of the world, AV systems must be capable of operating safely across different environmental and traffic conditions. The systems should be efficient

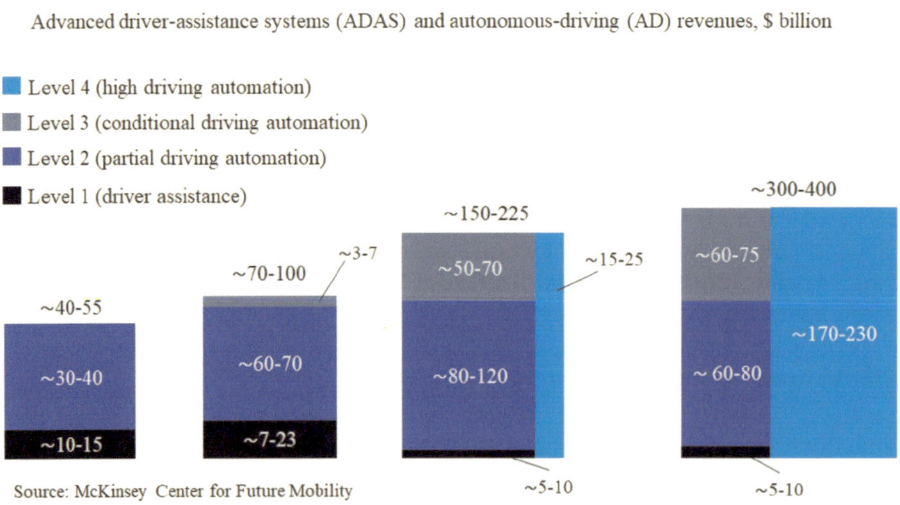

Figure 1.
ADAS market research report.

in delivering the objective of driving themselves considering the unpredictable behavior of the surrounding world.

2. *Efficient testing* – Traditional testing methods involve real-world driving which can be time-consuming, expensive, and might also be limited in the scope of scenario-based testing as the testing team can only perform a fixed number of scenarios with the actual vehicle in the given amount of time. To tackle this, the industry is moving toward simulation and virtual validation techniques. These allow for accelerated testing cycles with opportunities to create a vast number of scenarios. These virtual tests can include edge cases like complex traffic intersections and extreme weather, and all the regular ADAS features, thus making the development envelope larger while decreasing the costs and development time.

3. *Infrastructure* – The current road networks and communication infrastructures are not capable of supporting the advanced requirements of autonomous vehicles. While the sensors on these vehicles are advanced enough to provide comprehensive detection and interpretation of the surroundings, the sensors in the outside world need to be further developed to help in Vehicle-2-Everything (V2X) features. The road markings and traffic signs have to be maintained well throughout the lifetime which are crucial in providing necessary information to the sensors of the AV.

1.2 Introduction to the concept of scenario-based testing and virtual validation

Autonomous vehicles need to navigate safely through different traffic and environmental conditions. It can take a considerable amount of time to test all the possible scenarios with physical testing. To tackle this, *via* simulations, a wide variety of traffic scenarios, as well as different weather and illumination conditions, can be performed in an efficient manner. Engineers and developers can build the scenarios to be tested in the dedicated software, where a digital twin of the actual autonomous vehicle will be deployed and tested.

Scenario-based testing ensures that the AV systems can be rigorously tested across different sets of conditions, improving the performance of perception, planning, and control systems in various aspects. Virtual validation enables rapid iteration and assessments in the virtual environment which will bring down the development time and the related costs. This is achieved by using powerful computing systems to test multiple scenarios continuously where the developers can intervene to improve the controller algorithm or to calibrate the sensors.

Scenario-based testing provides evidence of the reliability and safety of AVs. Virtual validation further enhances this process by enabling continuous testing and iterative development without the additional time and expense of physical prototypes. Together, these help ensure that the AV technology is rigorously tested and refined, before deploying onto physical hardware.

1.3 Overview of proposed approach and main contributions

Siemens provides scalable solutions for safety validation with a portfolio of software tools and an integrated toolchain that complies with international regulations and standards. By using recorded data to extract critical scenarios and synthetically generate edge cases, the toolchain enables automatic and effective scenario synthesis. Taking care of the software infrastructure and adding scenario-generation elements expedites the validation procedure and reduces the safety hazards in ADAS and AV systems.

Siemens' approach for safety validation of automated vehicles is showcased in **Figure 2**. The workflow consists of different steps that commence with requirements management, followed by scenario extraction and creation, and finally the assessment phase. This workflow, together with the toolchain, systematically supports the scenario-based testing of ADAS and AV systems using Model-in-the-Loop (MiL), Software-in-the-Loop (SiL), and Hardware-in-the-Loop (HiL) setups.

The main contributions of this book chapter can be summarized as follows. Section 2 deals with deriving and managing the requirements. First, the applicable legislation as well as the relevant standards are highlighted. Next, the first steps of the overall workflow are described, starting with the description of the operational design domain, definition of the dynamic driving task and requirements management. All these steps, define requirements for data collection and scenario extraction/creation, which are described in next section.

Section 3 introduces a systematic approach to extracting known-safe scenarios from real-world data using Siemens' Simcenter Autonomy Data Analysis (ADA) tool. These scenarios serve as the foundation for further testing and optimization. Siemens' Critical Scenario Creation (CSC) tool innovatively transforms known-safe scenarios into high-risk scenarios, including known-unsafe and unknown-unsafe situations. The use of advanced optimization techniques for scenario creation addresses potential risks and improves testing comprehensiveness.

The toolchain incorporates standardized test scenarios from regulatory frameworks such as EURO NCAP, UN-R131, and ISO standards, ensuring compliance with safety and performance regulations for autonomous and advanced driver-assistance systems.

Section 4 presents the Siemens methodology and tooling for virtual scenario-based testing, including high-fidelity simulation models, advanced techniques for scenario selection and sampling, and methods for requirements coverage. The methodology and tooling are also discussed with respect to simulation credibility assessment frameworks, providing examples of usability and simulation models and results validation.

Section 5 discusses the verification and validation of ADAS and AV using simulation. In particular, Software-in-the-Loop (SiL) and Hardware-in-the-Loop (HiL)

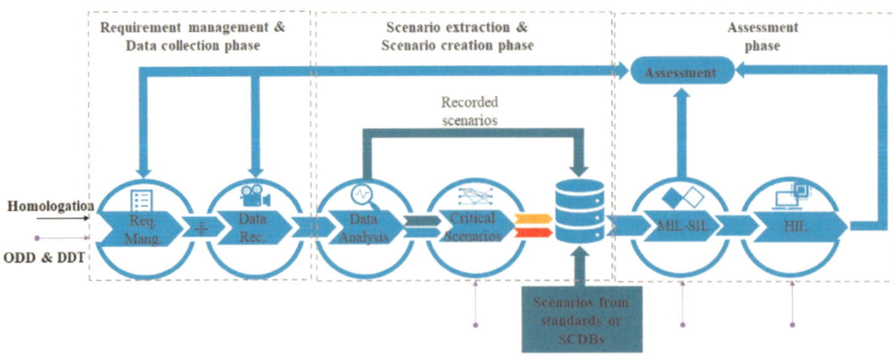

Figure 2.
Siemens autonomy toolchain and workflow for ADAS/AV.

environments and CCAM testing are discussed. The challenges of these setups are summarized and two examples of HiL simulations are given to illustrate these challenges and to propose solutions for them. Finally, Section 6 summarizes the main conclusions of this chapter.

2. Deriving and managing requirements for ADAS/AV

In this section first the applicable legislation and standards are discussed, then the operational design domain description is provided and finally, the importance of requirement management and tracking is discussed.

2.1 Applicable legislation and standards for ADAS/AV

In August 2022, the EU Commission adopted regulation 2022/1426 laying down rules for the application of regulation (EU) 2019/2144 of the European Parliament and of the Council as regards uniform procedures and technical specifications for the type-approval of the automated driving system (ADS) of fully automated vehicles.

The assessment of the automated driving system of fully automated vehicles, as proposed by this regulation, relies heavily on the traffic scenarios that are relevant to the different use cases of fully automated vehicles. It is therefore necessary to define those different use cases.

Given the complexity of automated driving systems, it is necessary to supplement the performance requirements and tests of this regulation with manufacturer documentation demonstrating that the automated driving system is free of unreasonable safety risks to vehicle occupants and other road users in the relevant scenarios and during the ADS lifetime.

In this sense, in February 2021, the United Nations Economic Commission for Europe (UN-ECE) presented the New Assessment/Test Method for Automated Driving (NATM) [4] – a framework, that introduces a multi-pillar approach for safety validation of automated driving, see **Figure 3**.

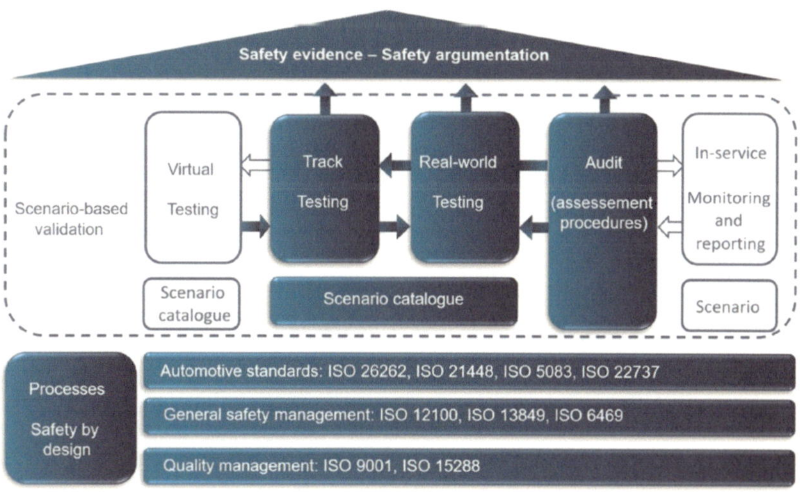

Figure 3.
Multi-pillar approach for safety validation of automated driving systems.

The multi-pillar safety validation of automated vehicles specifies five certification pillars, which support the safety argumentation. In addition to the three well-known pillars (track testing, real-world testing, and audit), the regulation mentions virtual testing and in-service monitoring.

In this document, the verification, validation, assurance, and certification are defined/described as follows:

- Verification is an activity that determines whether a system meets the requirements, answering the question: "Did we build the system right?"
- Validation is assessing if the system meets the end user needs, answering the question: "Did we build the right system?". On the other hand, model validation is evaluating how well the model represents reality.
- Assurance is justified confidence that the system functions as intended.
- Certification determines whether a system conforms to a set of criteria or standards.

In the next subsections, we briefly overview the most relevant standards.

2.1.1 ISO 26262: Functional safety standard

The ISO26262 functional safety standard is well-known and widely used in the automotive sector [5]. The standard lays down the main requirements of how the system should detect and respond to failures, errors, or off-nominal performance. As shown on the left side of **Figure 4** ISO 26262 defined several workflows such as product development at the system level, software development, and hardware development. Each workflow includes testing, verification, and validation activities.

The detailed software development workflow, including software integration and testing, verification of software safety requirements, system integration, and testing is presented in **Figure 4**, see right side.

2.1.2 ISO 21448: SOTIF

The ISO 21448 (SOTIF) – safety of the intended functionality – describes how the system should detect and respond to functional insufficiencies of the intended functionality or reasonably foreseeable misuse by persons [6].

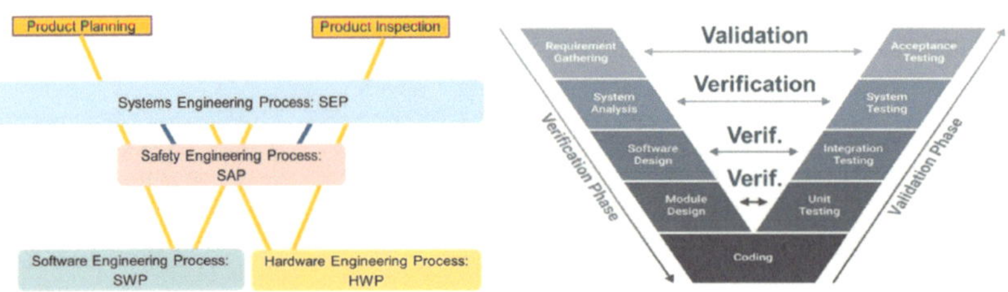

Figure 4.
Development workflow (left) and software development workflow (right) according to ISO 26262.

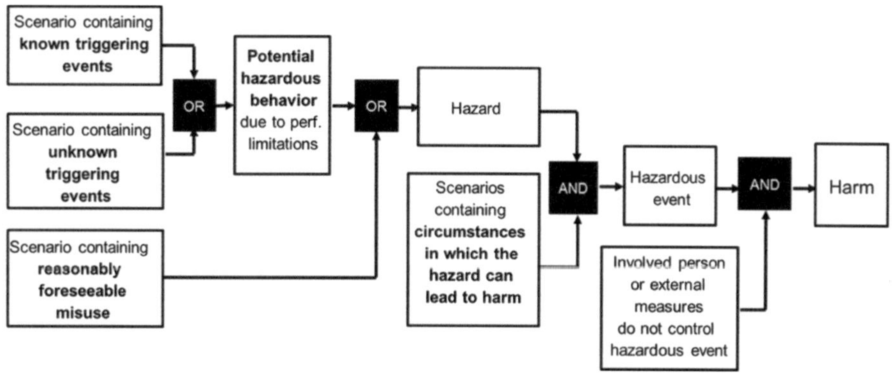

Figure 5.
Hazardous event model according to ISO 21448.

The objective is to validate the automated function in all relevant scenarios, especially under difficult conditions for both sensors and algorithms. As a remark: functional insufficiencies at the vehicle level due to - insufficiency of specifications (e.g., incorrect/incomplete specifications) - performance limitation (e.g., limited sensors range, overestimated braking assistance).

The end goal – SOTIF release – is the absence of unreasonable risk due to hazards resulting from functional insufficiencies of the intended functionality or by reasonably foreseeable misuse by road users. The hazardous event model according to ISO 21448 is presented in **Figure 5**.

ISO 21448 introduces the concept of scenario-based testing, where the scenario is defined as a sequence of scenes usually including the automated driving system(s) (ADS)/subject vehicle(s), and its/their interactions in the process of performing the dynamic driving task (DDT).

Furthermore, the scene is defined as a snapshot of all entities including, but not limited to the automated driving system (ADS)/subject vehicle, scenery, dynamic environment, and all actors and observer's self-representations, and the relationships between those entities. Finally, scenery is defined as part of the environment that remains unchanged.

According to ISO 21448, the development is a progressive process as shown in **Figure 6**. The scenario space is divided into safe and hazardous (non-safe) scenarios as well as known and unknown scenarios.

One of the major goals of the development according to ISO 21448 is to discover the unknown and hazardous scenarios and make them known and later by certain technical measures (e.g., by adapting the system under test of limiting the operational design domain) make them safe. Finally, the "area" of safe and known scenarios shall increase and the area of hazardous scenarios shall decrease significantly.

Other relevant standards, which are not detailed here, include ISO 22737 and ISO 34502. The ISO 22737 standard specifies low-speed automated driving (LSAD) system requirements and procedures, which are going to assist manufacturers of LSAD systems in the incorporation of minimum safety requirements in their designs and allow end users, operators, and regulators to reference a minimum set of performance requirements in their procurements [7].

ISO 22737 is a very clear and prescriptive standard, which can be used during the development of LSAD.

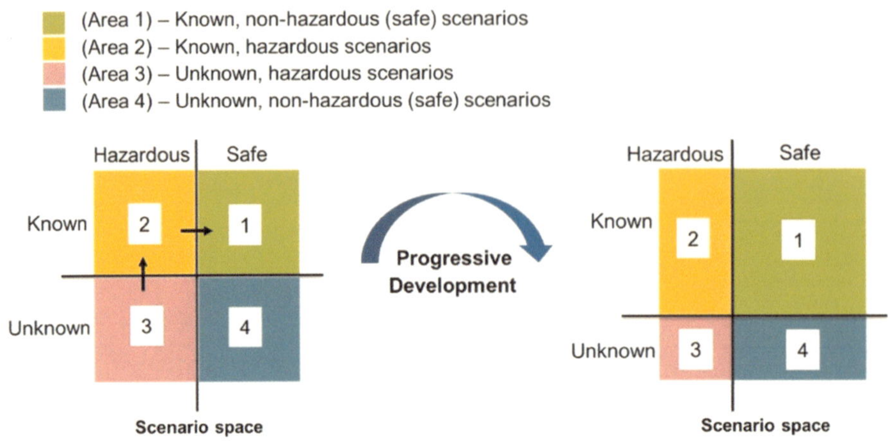

Figure 6.
Progressive development according to ISO 21448.

2.2 ODD description

A key aspect of the safe use of automated vehicle technology is defining its capabilities and limitations and clearly communicating these to the end user, leading to a state of "informed safety". The first step in establishing the capability of an ADS is the definition of its operational design domain (ODD). The ODD represents the operating environment within which an ADS can perform the dynamic driving task (DDT) safely.

As shown in Section 1.3 the verification and validation workflow starts with a description of ODD, a definition of the DDT, and requirements elicitation according to applicable legislation and standards, as shown in **Figure 7**.

In this subsection the focus is mainly on the ODD, the next subsection is related to requirements definition and requirements management, especially how the requirements are linked to the assessment. Based on the ODD definition and defined requirements the data collection/recording can start, which can feed the scenario generation as well as the model validation process.

The ODD taxonomy specified in this BSI PAS 1883 enables ADS manufacturers to specify and implement minimum safety requirements in their designs, and allows end users, operators, and regulators to reference a minimum set of ODD attributes and performance requirements in their procurements [8].

The ODD description is structured according to **Figure 8** left side and a so-called ODD checklist is included: see **Figure 8** right side which is a very important checklist during the design as well as testing of ADS.

It will also enable ADS manufacturers, developers, and suppliers of components and sub-components to define the operating capability and assemble sets of evidence that will improve confidence in the safety of the resulting product (such as component specifications) and in the data obtained from appropriate test and verification activities.

This BSI PAS 1883 document is intended for organizations developing safety cases for automated vehicle trials and testing, manufacturers and developers of Society of Automotive Engineers (SAE) Level 3 and SAE Level 4 ADS, and suppliers of components and sub-components. It is also of interest to insurers, regulators, service providers, and national, local, and regional governments to enable them to understand possible ADS deployments and capabilities.

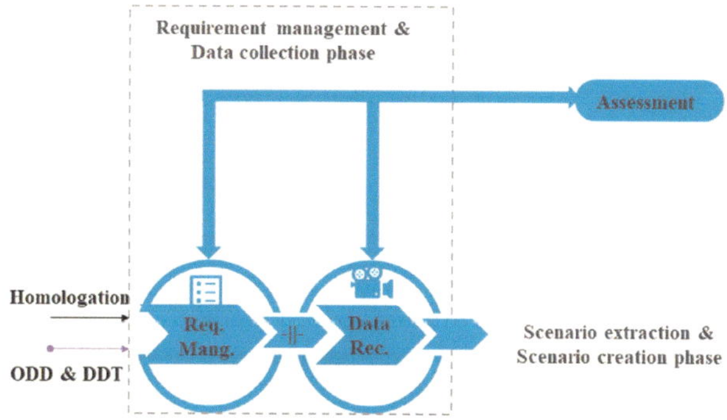

Figure 7.
The first steps of the workflow - requirements management and data collection.

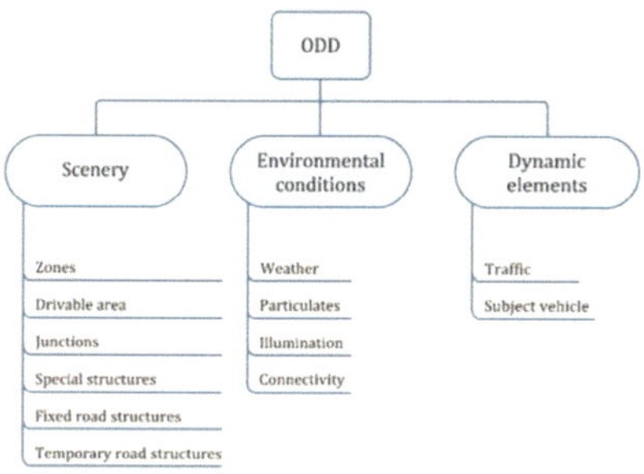

Attribute	Sub-attribute	Sub-attribute	Capability
Drivable area geometry	Horizontal plane	Straight roads	Yes
	—	Curves	Yes – up to 1/500 m (radius of curvature)
	Vertical plane	Up-slope	Yes
		Down-slope	Yes
		Level plane	Yes
	Cross-section	Divided/undivided	Divided
		Pavement	Yes
		Barrier on the edge	No
		Types of lanes together	Only traffic lane

Figure 8.
ODD description (left side) and ODD checklist (right side) according to BSI PAS 1883.

The BSI PAS 1883 document does not cover the basic test procedures for attributes of the ODD, the monitoring requirements of the ODD attributes, and the format of the ODD definition.

2.3 Requirements management

Before we start to discuss requirements management it is essential to define the main characteristics of well-written requirements. Well-written requirements shall have (at least) the following characteristics (see ISO 26262): complete, consistent, feasible, modifiable, unambiguous, and testable.

Complete: The requirements must be complete, meaning they shall contain all the required information to realize/implement the requirement. There is no need to assume anything to realize/implement the requirement.

Consistent: Consistent requirements mean that there is no contradictory information in the requirements document. Feasible: This is one of the crucial aspects of requirements. Requirements shall be implementable within the given time frame and budget and implementable using the existing and chosen technology platform.

Modifiable: In most projects, requirements are never static and do not stop after the requirements document is signed off. The best way to manage the requirements is to manage these changes using a requirements management tool. In case of any changes, the specific requirements and the dependent ones can be modified accordingly without impact on the others.

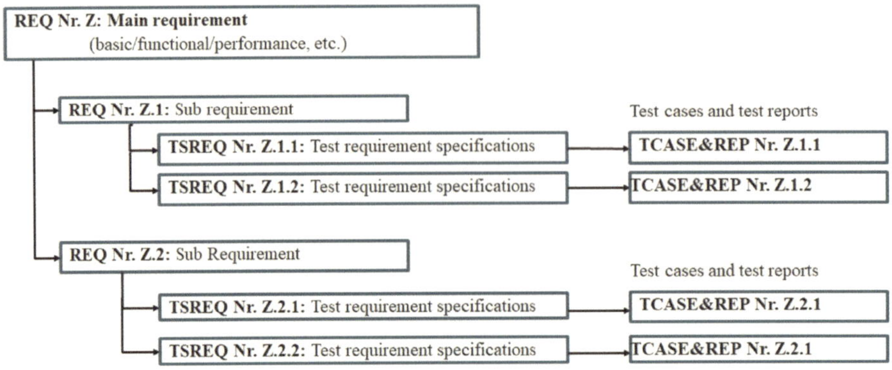

Figure 9.
Requirements, test requirements, test specifications, test cases, and test reports.

Unambiguous: Unambiguous means a single interpretation. If a requirement is defined so that it can only be interpreted in one way, it means it is unambiguous. All subjective words or statements must be eliminated from the requirements.

Testable: A testable requirement can be defined as a requirement, which can be tested and validated using any of the following methods: inspection, walk-through, demonstration, or testing.

Furthermore, the workflow associated with the virtual verification and validation methodology shall be traceable (see continuous integration/continuous deployment ISO 21448), platform-independent, scalable (shall be able to handle large amounts of data) and modular to handle high-complexity systems.

The requirements usually are grouped into main categories, like basic or general requirements, system requirements, functional safety requirements, performance requirements, etc. Furthermore, the requirements are split into sub-requirements, from which test requirements specifications and test cases are derived, see **Figure 9**. These links usually are created manually by the requirement engineer.

The requirements related to the virtual verification and validation (V&V) methodology shall clearly separate verification requirements and validation requirements.

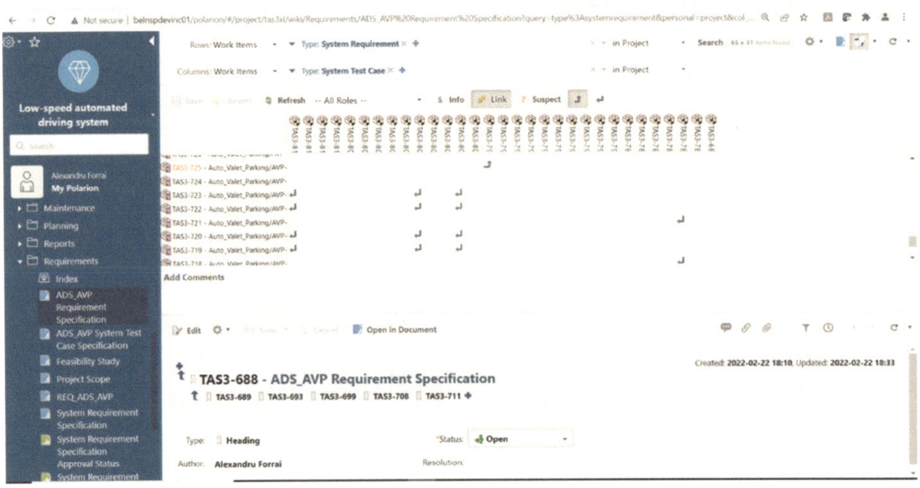

Figure 10.
Traceability matrix – linking requirements with test cases – example in polarion.

Requirements shall be linked to test cases, so traceability between requirements and test cases is established (see ISO 26262).

Subsystems and systems are verified against technical requirements (in line with the concept "doing things right") and subsystems and systems are validated against end user requirements ("doing the right things"), see ISO 26262.

By linking the requirements with the test requirements and test cases, a so-called traceability matrix is generated as shown in **Figure 10**, where a requirement shall be tested by at least one test requirement.

3. Scenario extraction and creation

This section outlines the process of extracting and creating scenarios for testing autonomous vehicle systems. First, known-safe scenarios are extracted from real-world driving data using the Simcenter ADA tool. These scenarios form the foundation for further testing.

To assess system performance under more challenging conditions, Siemens' Critical Scenario Creation (CSC) tool transforms known-safe scenarios into known-unsafe scenarios by optimizing risk factors. The CSC tool also creates unknown-unsafe scenarios through a three-step process involving feature extraction, behavior configuration, and risk identification, using advanced optimization techniques. Additionally, standard test scenarios from regulatory bodies are integrated to ensure compliance with safety protocols and regulations.

3.1 Data collection and data analysis

The data collection process begins by gathering information from various sources, including vehicle sensors, drone footage, and infrastructure-mounted devices, to capture real-world driving scenarios within the ODD. Siemens provides the necessary tools and services for sensor setup, data recording, and data processing.

This process ensures that actor behaviors, traffic flow, and other environmental elements are accurately captured and processed. Errors in the collected data, such as noise, missed detections, and occlusions, are corrected during data processing, which results in reliable and complete trajectory datasets.

In terms of data analysis, the Simcenter ADA tool is responsible for processing raw data and extracting known-safe scenarios. Simcenter ADA analyzes the data to extract, replay, and categorize scenarios, evaluating them based on key performance indicators (KPIs). Additionally, users can explore specific scenarios in detail and export the data for further simulation.

However, Simcenter ADA only extracts known-safe scenarios, which are essential for testing under noncritical conditions. These safe scenarios serve as a baseline for further critical scenario generation.

3.2 Scenario extraction

Scenario extraction is primarily handled by the Simcenter ADA tool, which identifies known-safe scenarios based on safety thresholds. These scenarios are carefully categorized to ensure that they meet the requirements. Known-safe scenarios are valuable for verifying system performance in stable, nonhazardous conditions.

To address critical testing needs, Siemens also employs its Critical Scenario Creation (CSC) tool, which builds upon the known-safe scenarios extracted by Simcenter ADA. The CSC tool is used to generate two types of high-risk scenarios: known-unsafe and unknown-unsafe.

3.3 Critical scenario creation

The Critical Scenario Creation (CSC) tool plays a crucial role in transforming known-safe scenarios into high-risk scenarios that are essential for testing autonomous vehicle systems in more dangerous and unpredictable situations.

- Known-unsafe scenarios: Based on the known-safe scenarios provided by Simcenter ADA, the CSC tool optimizes scenario parameters to identify potential risk factors. By increasing the criticality of the known scenario, the tool generates known-unsafe scenarios (shown by the orange arrow in **Figure 11**). These scenarios are critical for assessing how well autonomous systems handle predictable, hazardous conditions.

- Unknown-unsafe scenarios: The creation of unknown-unsafe scenarios involves a more complex process, as these scenarios represent unforeseen, potentially dangerous situations that may not have been previously encountered. The CSC tool provides a three-step process for unknown-unsafe scenario creation involves ([9, 10]):

1. Extraction: The first step is to extract key features that describe the behavior of actors in the scene, such as vehicle paths, velocity profile and offset to center of the lane. These features are determined by modeling the road layout as a graph and calculating probability distributions for each parameter and node combination. For actor i, the probability of behavior $P_{a,i}$ is computed as:

$$P_{a,i} = P_{p,i} \prod_{j=1}^{m} P_{par,j} \tag{1}$$

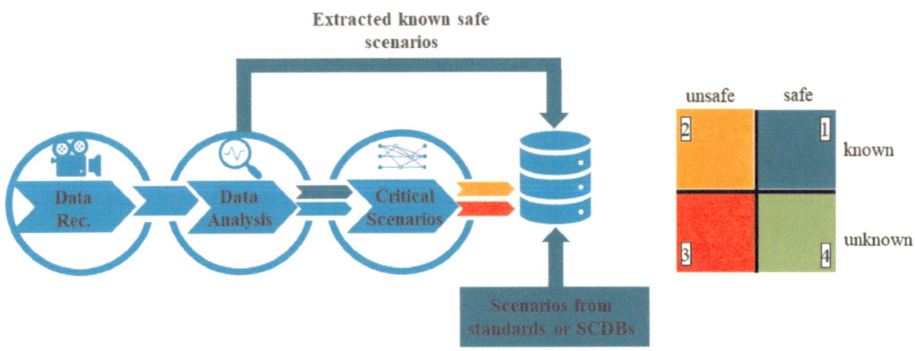

Figure 11.
SOTIF scenarios (right), Siemens autonomy toolchain for scenario generation (left), and arrows in green show scenarios from safe-known, orange, and red arrows show the known-unsafe and unknown-unsafe scenarios, respectively.

where:

- $P_{p,i}$ is the probability of a path cluster for actor i,
- $P_{par,j}$ represents the probability of the $j - th$ parameter,
- m is the number of parameters extracted for actor i.

1. Configuration: The next step is to configure the behavior of actors and parameters to define the search space. Given the complexity of the scenario, the tool automatically reduces the search space by identifying noninteracting actor paths with ego vehicle and partitioning the remaining space based on discrete parameters, for example, colliding actor type. This step reduces the search space, making it manageable for further optimization.
2. Identification: The final step involves applying an optimization algorithm to assess the risk and novelty of the generated scenarios. This step uses proprietary metrics to identify the most critical scenarios, focusing on time to collision (TTC) and unexpectedness. The unexpectancy is calculated based on the difference between what the ego vehicle predicts and what is happening in a scenario. The objective function $f(\eta)$, which evaluates the risk of a scenario (having scenario parameters η) is defined as:

$$f(\eta) = G(P_s(\eta))(2 - \epsilon(\eta) + TTC_{min}(\eta)) \tag{2}$$

where:

- $G(P_s(\eta))$ is a function of the scenario probability $P_s(\eta)$,
- $\epsilon(\eta)$ is an unexpectedness metric to measure novelty (with a constant of two added to ensure a nonnegative value),
- $TTC_{min}(\eta)$ represents the minimum time to collision.

The scenario probability $P_s(\eta)$ is calculated as:

$$P_s(\eta) = \lambda_{TL} \prod_{i=1}^{n} P_{a,i} \tag{3}$$

where:

- λ_{TL} is a factor in traffic lights,
- $P_{a,i}$ is the probability of actor behavior i,
- n is the number of actors.

The optimization problem is formulated to minimize the risk function $f(\eta)$, subject to constraints:

$$\min_{\eta} f(\eta) \qquad subject\ to \qquad \eta \in X, \zeta_{col} = 0 \tag{4}$$

where X defines the bounds for the scenario parameters, and ζ_{col} is a Boolean variable that is 0 in case of ego collision and 1 in case of non-ego actors collision. This approach allows the CSC tool to generate unknown-unsafe scenarios (as shown by the red arrow in **Figure 11**), which represent unforeseen, potentially dangerous situations. These scenarios provide critical insights into how autonomous systems respond to rare and unexpected hazards.

3.4 Standard scenarios

In addition to the scenarios generated through extraction and critical scenario creation, the Siemens toolchain also incorporates standardized test scenarios from various regulatory bodies and accident databases. These scenarios are based on industry-recognized standards, including:

- EURO NCAP (for Advanced Driver Assistance Systems, ADAS)
- UN R131 and UN R152 (Automated Emergency Braking Systems, AEBS)
- UN R157 (Automated Lane Keeping Systems, ALKS)

For autonomous vehicles, Siemens utilizes test scenarios specified by ISO standards, such as ISO 22737 (LSAD) and ISO/DIS 23374-1 (automated valet parking system), which provide guidelines for verifying and validating the performance of these systems in different driving environments. These standardized scenarios serve as a baseline for testing compliance with safety and performance regulations, ensuring that both ADAS and autonomous systems meet global safety requirements.

In addition to adhering to these regulations, the Siemens toolchain allows for the customization of scenarios based on expert input, enabling developers to test additional requirements specific to their operational design domain. These virtual tests help ensure the safety and robustness of the systems before they are subjected to real-world testing on roads.

4. Scenario-based testing: The workflow

In this section, the workflow for scenario-based simulation testing is described. **Figure 12** presents an example of a scenario-based testing workflow using the Siemens toolchain. The workflow begins with scenario selection from scenario databases (SCDBs) based on system under test (SUT) specifications, such as ODD and test requirements. This is followed by various techniques for scenario concretization and test automation. The ADAS/AV function is then evaluated against the concrete scenarios, and results are generated for the SUT assessment.

The Siemens toolchain provides the following key features to enable this workflow:

- Simcenter High-Performance Engineering Exploration and Design Optimization Software (HEEDS) [11] which provides test automation capabilities along with smart sampling and optimization methods.
- Simcenter Prescan [12] fully supports industry standards, ASAM OpenDrive [13] and OpenScenario-XML [14], for scenario description.

- Detailed and physics-based world model for representative sensor simulation. For example, measured materials are provided for accurate radar sensor simulation (e.g., to capture reflectivity and multi-path phenomena).

- Physics-based sensor simulation of ADAS/AV sensors and high-fidelity vehicle dynamics models.

- User-friendly APIs for incorporating ADAS/AV functions and external vehicle dynamics models for closed-loop scenario execution.

Building, configuring, and validating high-fidelity models for simulation is essential to ensure the reliability of simulation results. This is discussed in Section 4.1. The broader framework for the credibility of the simulation results, which includes model validation, is presented in Section 4.2. The final two subsections discuss scenario selection, sampling, and meeting coverage requirements for scenario-based testing.

4.1 Model building, model validation, and digital twins

Depending on the test scenarios and the underlying requirements, the fidelity required for the simulation models may be determined. Simcenter Prescan provides sensor models and vehicle dynamics models of different fidelity. For example, when testing perception functions, high-fidelity physics-based sensors may be used. On the other hand, when testing planning and control functions, ground truth sensor models or probabilistic sensor models which can output perception results with a certain error rate can be used.

The process of model building and model validation can be illustrated through the example of the physics-based camera (PBC) sensor simulation in Simcenter Prescan. The process of modeling can be separated into three parts: (a) the generic PBC model and camera sensor simulation, (b) configuration of the PBC model to a real camera, and (c) validation of the PBC model against the real camera.

The PBC model consists of a pipeline that models different layers of the physical sensor such as the lens and color filter array. The high-fidelity model can represent various physical effects that may occur, for example, geometric distortion, blooming, and flare. In conjunction with the camera model, the simulation engine must also accurately compute the propagation of light, including reflections, in the scene in different environmental conditions. Together, the physics-based simulation engine and PBC model enable accurate camera sensor simulation.

The high-fidelity PBC model provides many parameters, relating to different physical layers of the camera sensor, to configure the model for real camera sensors. Some relevant information for these parameters can be found in the technical

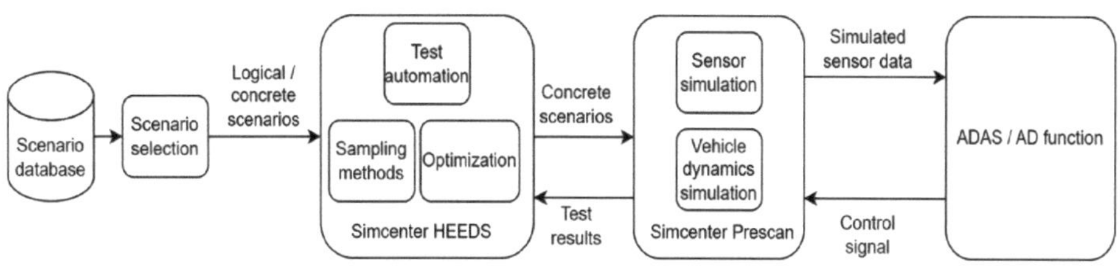

Figure 12.
Example scenario-based testing workflow.

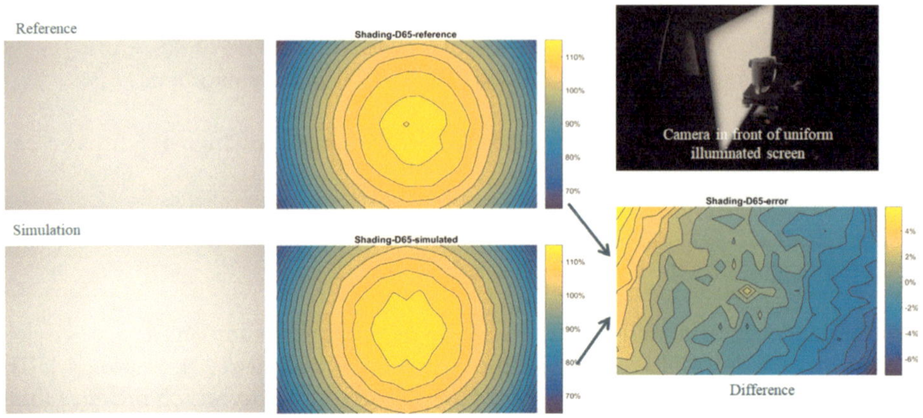

Figure 13.
Example validation of the PBC output against a real camera sensor. Here, the shading property of the camera image is being investigated.

specifications of the sensors. For some important properties, measurements in a laboratory are needed with the physical sensor. For example, a test setup is shown in the top right of **Figure 13**, where the camera is placed in front of a uniformly illuminated screen to understand the shading (or vignetting) properties of the camera.

The figure also shows how lab measurements are used for model validation. For this example, the vignetting behavior of the PBC in Simcenter Prescan is computed by recreating the laboratory test within the simulation. The vignetting behavior is then compared to the measured behavior of the physical sensor. Lab measurements may also be performed to validate sensor simulation under diverse weather conditions.

Additionally, the validation may be performed by evaluating the behavior of the target ADAS/AV camera processing pipeline on the camera simulation model outputs and the physical camera outputs. The test conditions chosen for validation should ideally cover the ODD sufficiently. It is important especially to focus on key factors known to impact the physical sensor and related AD functions, for example, weather and illumination.

4.2 Simulation credibility assessment

As simulation is an essential pillar of ADS safety assessment, it is important to assess and ensure the credibility of simulation results. Technical guidance on the credibility assessment of simulation-based testing is provided in the NATM [4] and the EU 2022/1426 regulation [15].

These documents provide a framework on credibility, which covers topics such as the suitability of the simulation models with respect to the ODD and assessment goals, and the correlation between simulation and physical testing. The credibility framework also includes the model building and model validation processes. These were already described in the previous section (Section 4.1). Below are two other aspects of how the Siemens toolchain conforms to the technical guidance in the above standards.

The usability pillar of the credibility framework includes documenting assumptions and limitations of simulation tooling and preventing incorrect use of the tools. The Simcenter Prescan manual and user graphical user interface (GUI) both provide such measures.

Consider the example of camera sensor simulation in rainy conditions. Firstly, the Simcenter Prescan user manual [12] details the theoretical foundations of the rain model, for example, principles governing the relationship between raindrop fall speed and raindrop diameter. The user is then guided to realistic values for the rain parameters, with recommendations are available also in the GUI. The user is further warned about limitations in accurately rendering the effect of light sources on the intensity of raindrops. To prevent incorrect use, a warning appears in the GUI, as described in the user manual:

> "In this release, weather (rain) is not directly influenced by car/street lights ... (this) will result in a parse warning"

To further demonstrate the simulation model validity, Siemens V&V methodology includes the use of hardware-in-loop testing and track testing to validate the simulation results. A subset of scenarios that have been tested in the simulation are used for a correlation analysis between simulation results and physical testing. The selection of the test scenarios sufficiently covers the ODD, but emphasizes key scenario regions:

- scenarios with results close to safety thresholds,
- known high variance regions of the simulator *(based on previous correlation studies, model validation, or known limitations of the simulator)*.
- safety-critical regions that are identified based on safety standards, for example, triggering conditions found during SOTIF safety analysis of the SUT.

4.3 Scenario selection and parametrization

The Siemens methodology and tooling include automatic retrieval of scenarios from scenario databases (SCDBs) based on use case specifications such as ODD and test requirements. This reduces manual effort and human error when searching SCDBs for scenarios.

For the universality of the tool, input and output formats must adhere to ISO 34503 (ODD taxonomy and specification) [16] and ASAM OpenLabel standards (scenario, behavior description) [17]. The input ODD definition must be specified as per ISO 34503 standard, while the input test requirements and the output query criteria are provided based on taxonomies of ISO 34503 and OpenLabel.

The tool is presented in **Figure 14**. Firstly, the natural language ODD definition (as per ISO 34503) is interpreted into a machine-readable format, and the requirements are parsed using the ISO 34503 ontology reference. Then, scenario query definition is performed per requirement, such that a traceable set of scenarios is obtained per requirement. Here, the test elements necessary based on the ODD and a requirement are identified.

For example, consider a requirement: *crossing traffic at intersections shall be detected by radar in dense fog* and an ODD definition including *fog: [clear, moderate, medium, dense]*. For this example requirement, dense fog is a relevant test attribute, and other ODD fog values are ignored. Once test elements are identified, a search query is generated and passed to the SCDB application program interface (API). The retrieved scenarios are provided to the user, and a traceability matrix is generated. The user is provided feedback when requirements are unclear or under-specified, such that the automated retrieval of scenarios is not possible.

The selected scenarios are then prepared for testing. Simcenter HEEDS provides test automation capabilities and advanced sampling techniques to efficiently test the SUT against the retrieved scenarios. For example, adaptive sampling iteratively samples the design space to increase test efforts in specific regions of interest within the parameter space, such as regions where the SUT behavior may change with smaller parameter steps.

Figure 15 shows how adaptive sampling efficiently approximates the response surface of a SUT in a cut-in scenario with two parameters: the SUT speed (horizontal axis) and cut-in vehicle speed (vertical axis).

The reference response surface (shown on the left) is obtained with an extensive grid-based sampling method. This response surface shows, as expected, that the SUT is unsafe when the ego vehicle has high speed and the cut-in vehicle has low speeds (top-left region of parameter space). However, unexpectedly, the SUT also behaves unsafely for high speeds of the cut-in vehicle (right-hand side of parameter space).

With a limited number of samples, adaptive sampling efficiently approximates the response surface; distinguishing unsafe regions from safe regions and detecting edge cases in the parameter space.

4.4 Assessment of scenario-based testing - workflow and requirements-based coverage

Safety argumentation for ADAS/AV requires test coverage for requirements. In this subsection, an example of effectively combining field testing and simulation-based testing is presented to meet coverage needs. **Figure 16** shows the process by which Simcenter ADA [18] extracts scenarios encountered by the SUT during field testing. A coverage analysis is then performed given the scenarios against the requirement verification plan. Gaps in requirement coverage (e.g., testing under diverse weather conditions) are then met through additional scenario generation or scenario retrieval from SCDBs as explained in the previous subsection. The additional scenarios are tested in simulation.

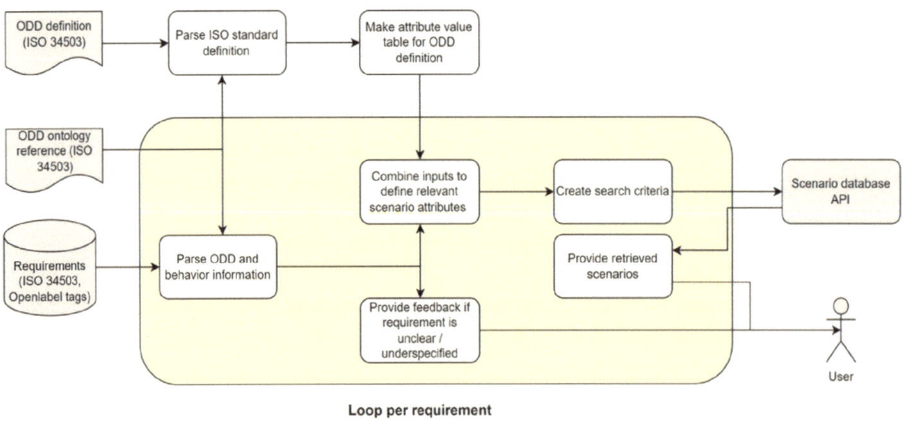

Figure 14.
Automated scenario retrieval from scenario databases.

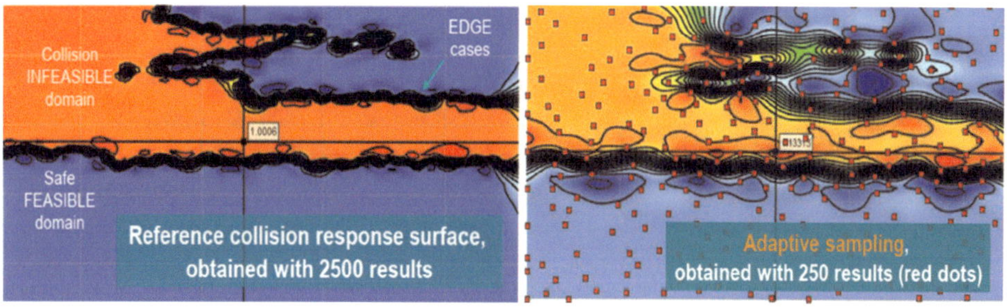

Figure 15.
The left figure shows a reference response surface of an SUT for a cut-in scenario, where the y-axis is SUT speed and the x-axis is cut-in vehicle speed. The blue region is safe, the red region is unsafe. The right figure presents the approximated response surface using Simcenter HEEDS adaptive sampling. The colors represent prediction confidence in safety, ranging from dark blue (safe with high confidence) to dark red (unsafe with high confidence).

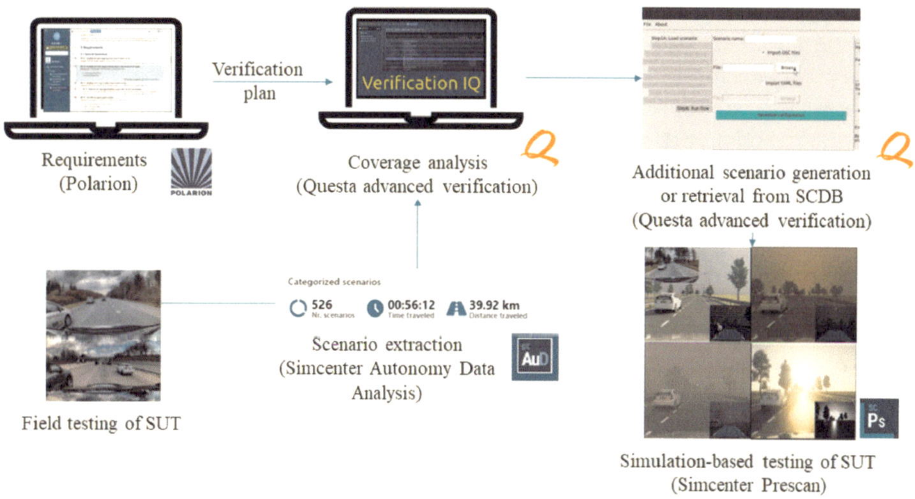

Figure 16.
Workflow for achieving requirements coverage by augmenting field testing with simulation-based testing. The Siemens tools enabling the workflow are mentioned in brackets.

For a full-scale and iterative V&V of ADAS/AV, a good test infrastructure with automated testing based on SUT updates, requirement management, and visualization dashboards to highlight coverage and assessment results is essential. The iterative V&V process often leads to new requirements and further developments of the SUT. The Siemens methodology and tooling presented in this section enable efficiently performing these V&V iterations and creating a solid safety argument for the SUT.

5. Virtual verification and validation

As became clear from the previous section, road vehicle automation functions, both for ADAS and AV, require extensive testing for verification of the requirements and validation of the resulting functionality, among others with respect to SOTIF. The assessment phase of Siemens autonomy toolchain is shown in **Figure 17**.

To enable this assessment efficiently, simulation environments play an important role. Various types of simulation environments exist, as explained in subsection 5.1. One of these is hardware-in-the-Loop (HiL), which is essential during assessment but generally poses one of the biggest technical challenges. This is elaborated upon in subsection 5.2, whereas subsection 5.3 provides two examples of HiL simulations.

Due to the inherent connectivity component in CCAM systems, testing these systems in a HiL-like environment requires specific measures, as further explained in subsection 5.4.

5.1 SiL and HiL testing

To reduce testing costs and time, a shift can be observed from real-world testing to virtual testing. The latter employs high-fidelity simulation models for the vehicle and its environment, while including the ADAS/AV control system in a phased approach, gradually moving from Model-in-the-Loop (MiL) *via* Software-in-the-Loop (SiL) toward the actual hardware implementation in a Hardware-in-the-Loop (HiL) setup following Siemens' toolchain as explained previously and also described in Ref. [19].

Whereas MiL simulations are primarily useful at the development phase of the automation function, SiL and HiL simulations target verification and regression testing of the automation function. Here, SiL focuses on efficiently checking compiled automation software deployed on the simulation platform, after which the next step is to check the actual hardware implementation of the compiled software in a HiL setup.

In the broader context of ADAS/AV development, these simulation architectures fit into the V-model development lifecycle, where HiL simulation bridges the gap between SiL testing and vehicle-level testing. It serves as a crucial intermediate step, allowing for the validation of both hardware and software components in a controlled, reproducible environment before moving to more expensive and complex vehicle prototypes.

To better understand the simulation setup involved in SiL and HiL, the basic logical architecture of a controlled vehicle (whether equipped with ADAS or with AV functions) in simulation is depicted in **Figure 18**. This figure shows the ego-vehicle model (the platform including actuators), which drives in a virtual environment, the latter including the static environment (road network, buildings, and other infrastructure), and the dynamic environment, that is, the other actors in the simulation. This virtual

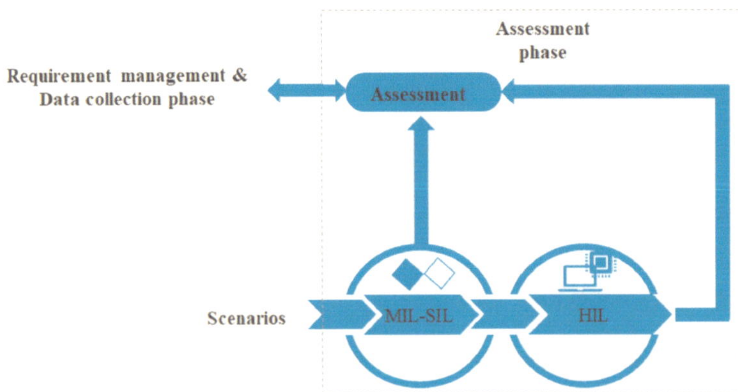

Figure 17.
Siemens autonomy toolchain - assessment phase.

environment is perceived by the ego-vehicle sensors such as lidar, radar, and camera. The output of these sensors as well as the output of vehicle dynamics sensors and, in the case of AV, a mission, constitute the inputs for the ADAS/AV automation software stack involving perception, planning, and control of the ego vehicle.

SiL simulation typically involves a compiled version of the automation software stack, running on a PC, whereas the other simulation components run in a simulation environment such as Simcenter Prescan. SiL simulation is particularly useful for detecting the following types of errors:

- Syntax errors, which already show up at compilation time;
- Runtime errors such as a memory leak, division by zero, and encoding errors;
- Semantic errors, that is, the automation software stack does not generate error messages, but the result of the computations is not what the programmer intended.

As such, SiL simulation serves to discover compilation problems, but not yet implementation problems. The latter is the focus of HiL simulation.

HiL simulation is a technique where real hardware components are combined with a virtual, simulated environment, thus establishing a hybrid testing environment. As ADAS/AV function software reaches the stage of deployment on target hardware, HiL provides a valuable environment for seamless integration and thorough testing of the target hardware in a simulated environment. As a result, HiL setups have become an indispensable tool in the development and testing of ADAS and AV functions.

One of the primary advantages of HiL setups is their ability to facilitate early testing, that is, when access to complete vehicle systems is yet limited or unavailable. By creating a virtual environment that simulates real-world conditions, HiL allows developers and engineers to conduct comprehensive tests, identify potential issues, and optimize performance well before the software is implemented in an actual vehicle, thereby saving time, effort, and costs associated with real-life testing on test tracks and public roads.

Additionally, risks associated with testing ADAS/AV software in real vehicles are minimized, ensuring a higher level of safety throughout the development process. Last but not least, HiL testing also allows for the exploration of edge cases and rare scenarios that might be difficult or dangerous to replicate in real-world testing. It is specifically this characteristic that makes HiL also useful for the verification and validation process after the ADAS/AV function design.

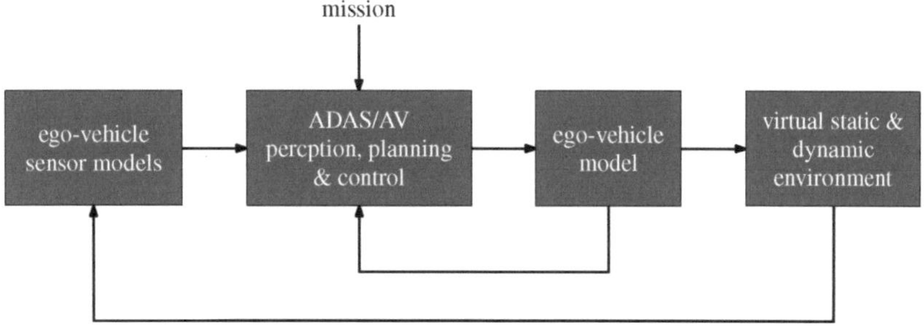

Figure 18.
High-level logical architecture of a vehicle equipped with ADAS/AV functionality in a simulation environment.

5.2 Challenges in HiL simulation

HiL simulations, however, involve several challenges, the most important of which are summarized as follows.

- *Scalability* — State-of-the-art vehicle automation systems employ complex and extensive sensor suites. For instance, Mobileye's SuperVision system [20] utilizes 11 cameras along with a long- and short-range radar sensor. Consequently, HiL setups for these systems must be capable of scaling easily to accommodate a multitude of simulated sensors while maintaining real-time performance.

- *Interfacing* — The hardware under test can be equipped with a large variety of interfaces, often sensor-specific. Examples are GMSL2 for cameras, CAN for radar, and automotive ethernet for lidar. Consequently, the HiL setup has to accommodate those interfaces, which can be considered as a specific aspect of scalability.

- *Synchronization* — Another challenge associated with multi-sensor systems, is the synchronization of data from multiple sensors. Each sensor may have different sampling rates and latencies, requiring algorithms to align the data streams accurately or at least ensure correct time stamping of all data. This synchronization is vital for testing sensor fusion algorithms and ensuring the ADAS/AV system receives a coherent representation of its environment.

To address the above challenges, in particular with respect to scalability, Simcenter Prescan has been designed to meet the demanding requirements of modern HiL setups. One of its key strengths is the inherent capability to be distributed across multiple nodes, providing a robust solution for scaling simulations to accommodate the increasing number of sensors in state-of-the-art ADAS/AV systems. This distributed architecture ensures that the simulation can maintain real-time performance.

Furthermore, Simcenter Prescan offers a powerful feature that allows users to insert custom code for manipulating sensor outputs directly on the GPU or CPU, referred to as User Algorithm on Federate (UAoF). This enables users to modify data streams or redirect them to generic PCIe devices, effectively simulating the physical signals of actual sensors. The ability to do this directly on the GPU or CPU reduces latency in the generation of the physical signals to meet real-time requirements. In summary, the foundations for scalability are created by

- The ability to deploy on multiple machines;

- A mechanism to stream sensor data from the simulation;

- The application of generic PCIe hardware interfaces.

5.3 HiL examples

This section presents two examples of HiL setups. Firstly, a so-called Injection HiL is presented, where simulated sensor signals are injected into an automation software stack running on an Electronic Control Unit (ECU). Secondly, a Projection HiL is described, involving a camera as hardware, detecting a simulated environment projected on a monitor.

5.3.1 Injection HiL

To illustrate the above considerations and the resulting HiL setup, **Figure 19** shows the hardware and software architecture of a setup to test the Apollo AV stack [21] implemented on a high-performance PC that mimics an onboard ECU.

Apollo performs localization, perception, routing, prediction and planning, and control. The inputs consist of vehicle dynamics sensors (termed 'chassis' in the figure), GNSS for vehicle location, and environmental sensor data (lidar and two forward-looking cameras in the figure). The outputs are throttle and brake level, and desired steering angle. Apollo utilizes a middleware layer called CyberRT, which is an open-source runtime framework that is highly optimized for performance, latency, and data throughput.

Next to the Apollo PC, the hardware also involves two PCs to simulate the ego vehicle and its environment using Simcenter Prescan. The first PC, termed Federate 1, simulates the ego vehicle in Simcenter Prescan (in combination with C++) by means of a multi-body Simcenter Amesim vehicle dynamics model, the static and dynamic environment, as well as a lidar model, being one of the onboard sensors.

The second PC, termed Federate 2, is dedicated to running both physics-based camera models since these are computationally intensive. To do so, Simcenter Prescan provides a mechanism to include the static and dynamic environment in Federate 2 during compilation time. Hence, at simulation time, only the actor motion needs to be communicated from Federate 1 to Federate 2 over a TCP connection, thereby reducing data transfer over the network.

Moreover, each camera model includes a UAoF to convert simulation data to the required format (which is RGB to YUV422 conversion in this case). Clearly, this

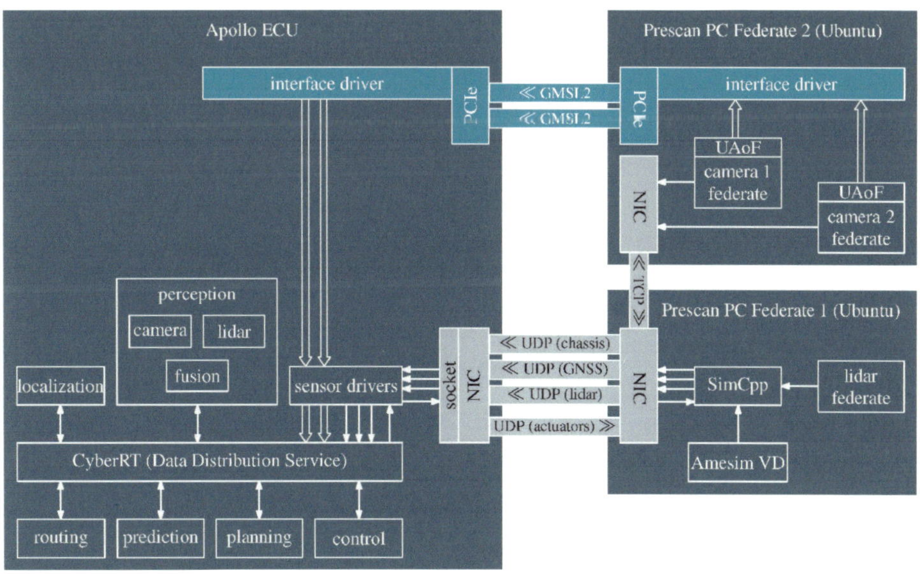

Figure 19.
HiL setup for evaluation of the Apollo AV control system in a virtual environment.

federated architecture introduces scalability with respect to the number of onboard sensors. In fact, any number of federated PC's can be added to run one or more sensor models, thus maintaining real-time execution when scaling up.

The schematic in **Figure 19** also shows the interfaces between the Simcenter Prescan simulation and the Apollo ECU. These interfaces conform to automotive standards, employing GSML2 for camera data and, in this example, UDP over automotive ethernet for lidar and vehicle dynamics sensors, indicated by the connected Network Interface Controllers (NICs) in the figure.

The GSML2 interface is implemented by dedicated PCIe boards. Due to the federated architecture and the UAoF capability, simulation data can be converted to any format that is required by the ECU hardware under test, thereby providing a highly generic setup, capable of accommodating a large variety of ECUs equipped with automotive-grade interfaces.

Finally, it is noted that all clocks in the HiL setup are synchronized with the Precision Time Protocol [22] (not shown in the figure). This allows the sensor fusion algorithm implemented in the ECU to correctly process all incoming sensor signals. Moreover, the Federate PCs execute the time update in a synchronized manner such that the ECU receives a coherent representation of its environment.

5.3.2 Projection HiL

Although HiL is usually associated with testing a hardware implementation of a decision and control system, it is also possible and useful to include other components of the system as depicted in **Figure 18** as hardware in a virtual environment. This is illustrated by the second HiL example, involving an automotive camera as the hardware under test.

The architecture of this HiL setup is shown in **Figure 20**, involving a simulated ego-vehicle, modeled in C++/MATLAB/Simulink, in a virtual environment provided by Simcenter Prescan. One of the ego-vehicle sensors, a camera, is included as hardware-in-the-loop. This camera is facing a monitor which displays the simulated static and dynamic environment. The CAN bus involves bi-directional

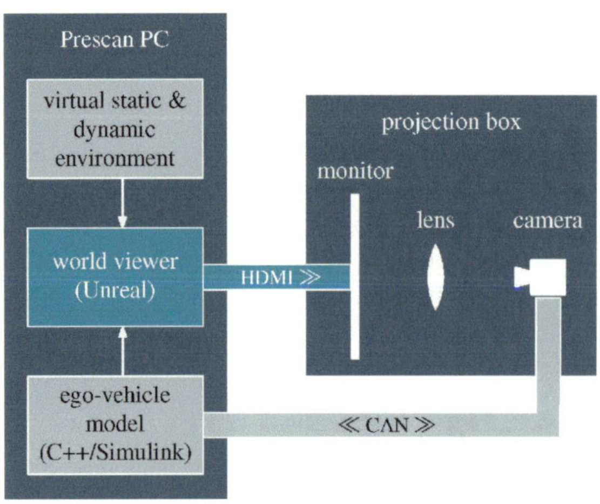

Figure 20.
HiL setup for evaluation of an automotive camera in a virtual environment.

communication, that is, communication of the detected object information to the Simcenter Prescan PC and communication of the ego-vehicle velocity to the camera.

Clearly, this HiL setup is less complex than the previous one. The issue of real-time simulation, however, is nevertheless present: In recent years, automotive cameras show significant improvement in terms of resolution and update rate, moving toward 4 K and 60 Hz, respectively.

Consequently, to provide a realistic simulated environment, the simulation must generate the image frames at the same or higher specifications. At the same time, environment visualization needs to resemble reality to an increasing extent over the past years, in particular, due to requirements imposed by AI-based image processing solutions.

As a result of these developments, the image generation involves an increasing computational effort. To significantly relieve this computational burden, Simcenter Prescan includes the feature of Deep Learning Super Sampling (DLSS), developed by NVIDIA [23]. This feature allows for generating camera frames at a lower resolution, thereby decreasing the rendering effort, after which the required resolution is obtained by low-effort up-sampling using a neural network.

The newer versions of DLSS add AI-based frame generation to the super sampling feature. This involves generating a new frame between two existing frames, hence doubling the update rate. As a result, the images can still be generated according to ever-increasing specifications.

5.4 CCAM testing

Remote monitoring is an essential feature of AVs and CCAM, for monitoring the ODD, performance, and safety monitoring of the automated driving system as well as for monitoring the traffic and the infrastructure. The autonomous vehicles can benefit from being remotely monitored so that if needed, the engineers and developers can look into the recordings and improve the driving performance of the vehicles.

Figure 21 shows the modular approach for remote monitoring. The two systems communicate with each other over the Message Queue Telemetry Transport (MQTT) cloud network.

The vehicle sends image frames, GPS coordinates, and other sensor information to the MQTT cloud. The local server, digital twin (DT) service runs programs to receive the data from the cloud, decode the data, and provide relevant visualization along

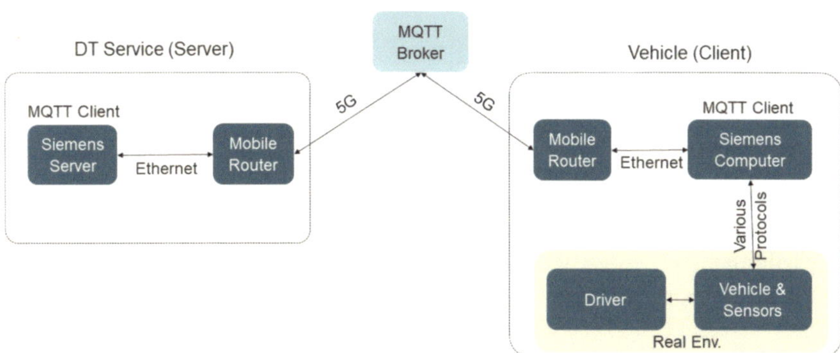

Figure 21.
Remote monitoring essential feature of CCAM and AV.

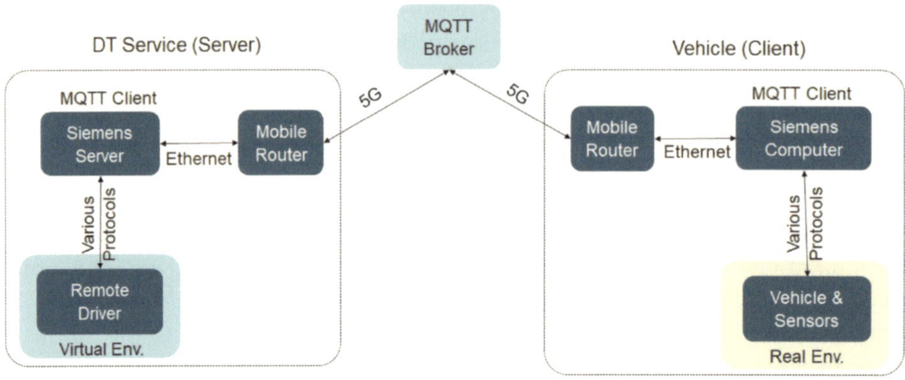

Figure 22.
Remote/tele-operated driving essential feature of CCAM and AV.

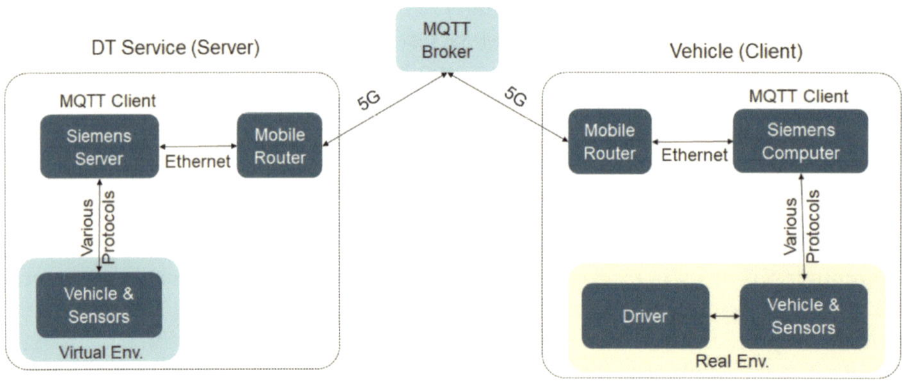

Figure 23.
Mixed-reality testing feature of CCAM.

with data saving options. The vehicle, its surroundings, including the infrastructure are all remotely monitored via the vehicle's onboard sensors see lower-right part of **Figure 21**. This real-time data, in combination with digital twins, can be used by the engineers to assess the vehicle safety/performance and improve/update the software whenever is necessary [3, 24].

The modular setup shown in **Figure 21** can be extended to remote/tele-operated driving, as presented in **Figure 22**. The remote driver perceives the images, GPS data, and provides input (acceleration/braking/steering) values to the remote vehicle *via* the MQTT cloud. The remote driver operates in a virtual environment and the vehicle is in the real-world environment, see **Figure 22**.

Remote monitoring - using advanced and safe communication networks with low latency - is an essential sub-component of the safe teleoperation, where the latter is mainly used during emergency maneuvers of AVs.

The presented applications in this subsection are essential features of CCAM and AVs, so proper testing and suitable test environments are necessary before deployment.

The mixed-reality testing setup shown in **Figure 23** allows testing efficiently and safely different scenarios in combination with V2X (e.g., roadside unit sensors), where virtual V2X objects are created in the virtual environment and can be injected remotely *via* the MQTT cloud, directly into the vehicle CAN bus.

Additionally, the setup allows to testing CCAM applications in the presence of packet loss, communication jitter, and different values of communication latency.

6. Conclusion

This chapter highlighted that the complexity of ADAS/AV requires efficient and robust testing methods to ensure safety and reliability. In this sense Siemens' autonomy workflow and toolchain for testing and virtual validation of ADAS/AV functions was presented.

The introduction section described the growing ADAS and AV market, driven by the integration of advanced technologies and increasing global demand. It addressed the main issues that AV development faces, like guaranteeing scalability, improving testing effectiveness, and getting around infrastructure constraints. The section highlighted virtual validation and scenario-based testing as effective testing of AV systems in a variety of circumstances. Siemens' toolchain was further presented for scenario generation and validation to speed up development.

In Section 2 we focused on the verification and validation workflow starting with describing the ODD, the definition of the DDT, and requirements elicitation according to applicable legislation and standards. In this sense, a detailed overview of the applicable legislation and relevant standards is provided. Furthermore, the requirements management process highlighted the importance of traceability between requirements and test cases/results.

Furthermore, the combination of known-safe scenario extraction and the generation of both known and unknown-unsafe scenarios ensures robust testing of autonomous vehicle systems, addressing both predictable and unforeseen hazards are discussed in Section 3.

The integration of standard scenarios from regulatory and industry standards highlights the features of the toolchain meeting global safety and performance requirements. In addition, advanced techniques in unknown-unsafe scenario creation enable developers to identify critical risks, ensuring improved system safety and reliability in complex and rare real-world scenarios.

In Section 4 we highlighted key components of the Siemens methodology and tooling for efficient, full-scale virtual scenario-based testing, including high-fidelity simulation models, automated scenario selection, advanced scenario sampling methods, and methods for requirements coverage.

It also demonstrated how the methodology and tooling conform with aspects of the simulation credibility assessment frameworks of NATM and EU 2022/1426 and how a solid safety argument based on virtual scenario-based testing can be achieved.

Finally, in Section 5, as an essential part of the verification and validation workflow, SiL and HiL simulation environments were discussed. Especially for HiL simulations, three challenges were presented, being scalability with respect to the number of simulated sensors, automotive-grade interfacing to make the gap toward actual implementation as small as possible, and synchronization of the various simulation components to ensure deterministic execution of the simulation.

It was shown that scalability is obtained by implementing a federated architecture of the simulation, thereby ensuring real-time execution independent of the number of simulated sensors.

In addition, essential CCAM and AV features, such as remote monitoring and tele-operated driving have been presented and a modular/distributed test environment has been described.

Acknowledgements

Co-funded by the European Union 6GSNS

HORIZON JU Innovation Actions - 101139048 - ENVELOPE - HORIZON-JU-SNS-2023. This project has received funding from the European Union's Smart Networks and Services Joint Undertaking (SNS JU) under grant agreement no. 101139048. Views and opinions expressed are however those of the author(s) only and do not necessarily reflect those of the European Union or SNS JU. Neither the European Union nor SNS JU can be held responsible for them.

Funded by the European Union NextGenerationEU Digital Infrastructure for Future-proof Mobility

This project has received funding from the European Union in the NextGenerationEU program under grant agreement no. NGFDI2201, Digital Infrastructure for Future-proof Mobility (DITM).

Funded by the European Union NextGenerationEU SUNRISE

This project has received funding from the European Union's Horizon Europe Research and Innovation Actions under grant agreement no.101069573, a safety assurance framework for connected, automated mobility systems (SUNRISE).

Author details

Alexandru Forrai*†, Mohsen Alirezaei†, Tajinder Singh†, Amit Gali† and Jeroen Ploeg†
Siemens Industry Software Netherlands B.V., Helmond, The Netherlands

*Address all correspondence to: alexandru.forrai@siemens.com

† These authors contributed equally.

References

[1] Markets and Markets. Advanced driver assistance systems market report. 2030. Available from: https://www.marketsandmarkets.com/Market-Reports/driver-assistance-systems-market-1201.html [Assessed: January 30, 2025]

[2] McKinsey and Company. Autonomous driving's future: Convenient and connected. Available from: https://www.mckinsey.com/industries/automotive-and-assembly/our-insights/autonomous-drivings-future-convenient-and-connected [Assessed: January 30, 2025]

[3] Forrai A, Gali A, Barosan I. Application of digital twins for connected, cooperative and automated mobility. In: IEEE Third Conference on Information Technology and Data Science, Debrecen. New York, USA: IEEE; 2024. pp. 44-50

[4] UNECE. The new assessment/test method for automated driving (NATM). Available from: https://unece.org/sites/default/files/2024-02/ECE_TRANS_WP.29_2022_58e.pdf [Accessed: January 30, 2025]

[5] ISO 26262 Road Vehicles. Functional Safety. 2nd ed. Geneva, Switzerland: ISO; 2018

[6] ISO 21448 Road Vehicles. Safety of the Intended Functionality. 1st ed. Geneva, Switzerland: ISO; 2022

[7] ISO 22737. Low-Speed Automated Driving (LSAD) Systems for Predefined Routes. 1st ed. Geneva, Switzerland: ISO; 2021

[8] BSI PAS 1883. Operational Design Domain (ODD) Taxonomy for an Automated Driving System (ADS) – Specification. 1st ed. London, UK: BSI (British Standards Institution); 2020

[9] Singh T, van Hassel E, Sheorey A, Alirezaei M. A systematic approach for creation of SOTIF's unknown unsafe scenarios: An optimization based method. In: SAE Technical Paper. Pennsylvania, USA: SAE International; 2024

[10] Rajesh N, van Hassel E, Alirezaei M. Unknown-unsafe scenario generation for verification and validation of automated vehicles. In: IEEE 26th International Conference on Intelligent Transportation Systems (ITSC). New York, USA: IEEE; 2023

[11] SIEMENS. Simcenter HEEDS. Available from: https://plm.sw.siemens.com/en-US/simcenter/integration-solutions/heeds/ [Accessed: November 25, 2024]

[12] SIEMENS. Simcenter Prescan. Available from: https://plm.sw.siemens.com/en-US/simcenter/autonomous-vehicle-solutions/prescan/ [Accessed: November 26, 2024]

[13] Association for Standardization of Automation and Measuring Systems. ASAM OpenDrive. Available from: https://www.asam.net/standards/detail/opendrive/ [Accessed: October 26, 2024]

[14] Association for Standardization of Automation and Measuring Systems. ASAM OpenScenario. Available from: https://www.asam.net/standards/detail/openscenario/ [Accessed: October 26, 2024]

[15] European Union. Uniform procedures and technical specifications for the type-approval of the automated driving system (ADS) of fully automated

vehicles. Available from: https://eur-lex.europa.eu/legal-content/EN/TXT/?uri=CELEX:32022R1426 [Accessed: October 10, 2024]

[16] International Standards Organization. ISO 34503:2023. Available from: https://www.iso.org/standard/78952.html [Accessed: June 15, 2024]

[17] Association for Standardization of Automation and Measuring Systems. ASAM OpenLabel. Available from: https://www.asam.net/standards/detail/openlabel/ [Accessed: June 18, 2024]

[18] SIEMENS. Simcenter autonomy data analysis. Available from: https://plm.sw.siemens.com/en-US/simcenter/autonomous-vehicle-solutions/autonomy-data-analysis-solution/ [Accessed: November 27, 2024]

[19] Alirezaei M, Forrai A, Tong S, Singh T. Siemens toolchain for testing and virtual validation of ADAS/AV functions. ATZ Magazine Worldwide. 2024;**126**:16-21. DOI: 10.1007/s38311-024-1948-x

[20] Mobileye. SuperVision. Available from: https://www.mobileye.com/solutions/super-vision [Accessed: November 25, 2024]

[21] Baidu Apollo. Apollo open platform. Available from: https://developer.apollo.auto [Accessed: November 25, 2024]

[22] IEEE standard for a precision clock synchronization protocol for networked measurement and control systems. In: IEEE Std 1588–2019 (Revision of IEEE Std 1588-2008), 16 June 2020. New York, USA: IEEE; 2024

[23] NVIDIA. DLSS. Available from: https://developer.nvidia.com/rtx/dlss [Accessed: November 25, 2024]

[24] Abdelsalam M, Forrai A. A design methodology for compositional simulation: The digital-twin interconnect framework. In: 23rd Driving Simulation and Virtual Reality Conference and Exhibition, Strasbourg, France, 2024, Product Solutions. Strasbourg, France: DSC2024; 2024. pp. 1-4